Individuals All

Individuals All

Perle Epstein

CROWELL-COLLIER PRESS, NEW YORK, NEW YORK
COLLIER-MACMILLAN PUBLISHERS, LONDON

The Macmillan Company, 866 Third Avenue, New York, N.Y. 10022
Collier-Macmillan Canada Ltd., Toronto, Ontario

Library of Congress catalog card number: 72-77277
Printed in the United States of America

Grateful acknowledgment is made to the following for permission to quote from copyrighted material: George Allen & Unwin Ltd. for passages from *Nigger: An Autobiography* by Dick Gregory with Robert Lipsyte, Copyright © 1964 by Dick Gregory Enterprises, Inc. Doubleday & Company, Inc., and Dick Gregory for passages from *The Shadow That Scares Me* by Dick Gregory, Copyright © 1968 by Dick Gregory. E. P. Dutton & Co., Inc., for passages from *Nigger: An Autobiography* by Dick Gregory with Robert Lipsyte, Copyright © 1964 by Dick Gregory Enterprises, Inc.; published by E. P. Dutton & Co., Inc. Farrar, Straus & Giroux, Inc., for passages from *Seeds of Destruction* by Thomas Merton, Copyright © 1961, 1962, 1963, 1964 by the Abbey of Gethsemani. Harcourt Brace Jovanovich, Inc., for passages from *The Seven Storey Mountain* by Thomas Merton, Copyright 1948 by Harcourt Brace Jovanovich, Inc.

This book is dedicated to

Lonnie
Todd
Dean
Julie
Susan
Cheryl
Ronald
Melanie
Neil
Donna Jo
Randy
Gabrielle

. . . and especially Hope, who asked for it to begin with

Acknowledgments

Thanks are due for their assistance, both professional and beyond the call of duty, to Miss Marian Boben and Mrs. Jean Adams of the Wolfsohn Memorial Library, King of Prussia, Pennsylvania; for his enlightening conversation about Thomas Merton, to Mr. Edward Rice; and to the Reverend James R. McGraw for his informative reminiscences and for reading the chapter on his friend Dick Gregory in the midst of writing his own book. Special thanks to Mae Feinstein for her generous assistance in typing the manuscript.

Contents

Individuals All

Henry David Thoreau

I am a Schoolmaster—a Private Tutor, a Surveyor —a Gardner, a Farmer—a Painter, I mean a House Painter, a Carpenter, a Mason, a Day-Laborer, a Pencil-Maker, a Glass-paper Maker, a Writer, and sometimes a Poetaster. . . . For the last two or three years I have lived in Concord woods alone, something more than a mile from any neighbor, in a house built entirely by myself.

Henry Thoreau was a rebel who never really left home; who never engaged actively in causes; who led hardly anyone but a few close friends—on nature walks rather than on strikes; who spent only one night in jail—all this despite the radical nature of his antislavery opinions, the anarchistic arguments in his essay *On Civil Disobedience*, and his highly individual life style. Thoreau was, in his life habits, a sort of New England yogi who could sit for hours in meditation before the door of his forest hermitage. He wrote: "Depend upon it that, rude and careless as I am, I would fain practice the Yoga faithfully. . . . To some extent, and at rare intervals, even I am a Yogi."

But he was a Harvard Yogi with a fine classical education, a well-informed naturalist, a translator of Latin poetry, and, in his shabby trousers and worn jackets, a rather eccentric intellectual.

He thought of himself as a philosopher. His neighbors regarded him as a crank. In his retreat at Walden Pond, Thoreau studied the great Indian classic, the *Bhagavad Gita*. He could hardly have imagined then that his essay *On Civil Disobedience*, along with the *Bhagavad Gita*, would have a profound influence on a twentieth-century Indian leader in his nonviolent rebellion against the British. It was a fair exchange for the transcendental pattern of life which Indian philosophy provided for Henry in his youth. Although he was a loner all his life Thoreau inspired causes ranging from nudism and vegetarianism to the most active and wide-ranging social reform. He himself shunned joining any groups, even those close to his heart, which were springing up all around him. Wildlife of any variety was more exciting to him than the constricting chatter and stuffy lecture halls of the reformers. He wrote articles for progressive magazines, and sometimes he could even be persuaded to attend Transcendentalist Club meetings, but not often. One stinging word from the skinny young man with the umbrella could too easily antagonize someone as sensitive to criticism as Margaret Fuller, professional lady revolutionary.

Like all perfectionists, Thoreau acted as a gadfly for the hypocritical community of socially integrated people around him. He passionately despised the materialistic business culture of America. He had watched too many Irish railroad workers starve in their shanties, and apparently could never forget the sight of runaway slaves being shipped back to their owners by church-going Bostonians. His perfectionism kept him from looking the other way, even at great discomfort to himself. Hence, despite the fact that he resigned from his family's church, and could be seen taking a nice long stroll in his shabby old clothes on a Sunday morning, he practiced the original teachings of that church in the actual business of his daily life. "The Church! It is eminently the timid institution, and the heads and pillars of it are constitutionally and by principle, the greatest cowards in the community."

People clucked their tongues at Thoreau's behavior: a Harvard graduate with no job and nothing to show for his family's efforts but boxes of butterfly specimens and dried leaves and notebooks filled with his observations of nature and man. His two years at Walden were a conscious, almost scientific experiment. Henry did not run away from home; on the contrary, he entertained his family in his hut and periodically brought his dirty laundry home for his mother to see about. On many occasions, after hearing the Emerson dinner bell ring just across the field from the pond, he would join them at their table; and many a morning he could be found at the town cobbler's, where he had taken his shoes to be soled.

Scholars are now digging deeper into the secrets of his psychology. Why exactly did he choose life in the woods at a specific time? Who could be responsible—a woman perhaps? Thoreau's romantic life is largely unknown. The sister of a Concord friend is reported to have said that she would as soon take his arm as take the arm of an oak tree. Ellen Sewall, a young lady visitor in the Thoreau home, turned down both his and his brother John's proposals of marriage; and he supposedly harbored a silent passion for Lidian Emerson, his friend's second wife. Some have suggested that his ambivalent attachment to his mother prevented him from relating completely to other women. Others claim that Mother Nature substituted for marriage and love. All of this is possible, but it does not change the fact that it was in his retreat that his great literary masterpiece, *Walden*, was born. It was here, too, that he did what all his Christian neighbors preached but did not practice: He gave up all material possessions and lived quite literally from day to day. "I found that, by working about six weeks in a year, I could meet all the expenses of living. The whole of my winters as well as most of my summers, I had free and clear for study."

At Walden Pond, in a hut built for and by himself at the cost of $28.12, he observed nature at close range, wrote, hoed beans, and tamed wild animals from July 4, 1845, to September 1847. He carved some of his own furniture and picked up the rest for nothing. He ate what he planted, sold what he could not use himself and bought what he could not grow. Eight months' worth of clothing, fuel, and other necessities cost him $10.40, and he still came out $2.82 ahead. He owned only the barest utensils; he left the door of his hut always unlatched, and was robbed only once—of a book by Homer. All in all, he considered his experiment a success. Confronting life at its most primitive not only afforded him the pleasure of proving his contention that most men live lives of quiet desperation, but for a long while it probably kept him free of the family tuberculosis that eventually killed him.

Henry Thoreau was a gentle man with animals and children, and a harsh man with sophisticated reformers, businessmen, and cultivated ladies. His taste for raw and uncompromising people later brought him to a heated defense of John Brown, whom he believed to be above the state slavery laws and beyond judgment. He never knew much about Brown's bloody career in Kansas, but saw and admired only the noble purpose and simple, un-affected pioneering strength of the old man. Yet Henry turned up his nose at Brook Farm, an experimental com-mune in Massachusetts, and had no use for reformers who spent their energies tending to the lives of others while their own lay fallow underneath them. For him, life was "for to admire and for to see." Most men, as far as he was concerned, lived only for the "blind and un-manly love of wealth," from which he turned his face completely. Thus with his big nose, short stature, yellow hair, and bright blue eyes, he made himself an unwel-come figure in many circles.

Thoreau's chosen isolation left him free to fill his note-books—an occupation adopted at the suggestion of Emer-son, his mentor and friend. Reports indicate that for a time Henry (who was fourteen years younger) emulated

Emerson in every other way as well: his voice, his manner, even his handwriting could hardly be distinguished from that of his friend. But by 1848 Henry began to find Emerson too elegant for his own simple tastes, too much of a patronizing conformist to suit him. And he went his own way. He preferred a vegetarian diet and an ascetic discipline of the body, which included nude bathing in the cold early morning waters of Walden Pond. In the afternoons he leaped into his boat and played the flute to the setting sun. One day he hoped to compile a book on the American Indian, even going so far as to learn some of their languages from guides and trappers. But though he left about three thousand pages of notes, he did not live to complete the task.

His few excursions were inexpensive, to say the least. For example, a trip to Canada and back cost him $12.75, including the price of two guide books. Thoreau always said it was best to travel in your oldest coat, overalls, and unpolished boots—probably because he often slept on the ground in open air, and because a hiker's roads were usually dusty. With ever-present umbrella, knapsack, music-book, field glass, measuring-tape, fish line, spoon and dipper, salt, sugar and tea, Indian meal, and a slice of fruit cake, he once walked from Concord to Provincetown.

Of all the members of the famous "Concord Group" of mid-nineteenth-century intellectuals, Thoreau is the only native. He was born in that town on July 12, 1817, into a family of French, Scotch, and English ancestry.

His father, John, did not do well in his business ventures until late in life when he settled down to making pencils. Henry was later to work on and off in his father's factory, at one point even inventing a fine new type of pencil made of graphite. People suggested that he patent his invention, but, uninterested in making a personal fortune, Henry remained contented with manufacturing his new pencils for his father. It was probably the graphite dust that activated the latent family tuberculosis of the Thoreaus.

Cynthia Thoreau, his mother, was a lively, intelligent woman who became popular as the leading Concord gossip. She dominated her shy, retiring husband and led the household, which was always filled with rent-paying aunts and lady boarders in addition to Henry's older brother, John, and two sisters, Helen and Sophia. John is noted to have been the brightest of the children, while at an early age Henry's sober and solemn mien earned him the title of "the judge." Nevertheless it was Henry who was chosen to attend Harvard College, while the rest of the family went to work in order to send him there. From the Concord Academy, a fine college preparatory school, he moved on to Harvard, only sixteen miles from home, in the year 1833.

Here he was known as an excellent student and a friendly person, though given to taking long walks by himself. In his junior year he became ill and went on a leave of absence, during which he worked as a tutor for the children of Unitarian minister Orestes Brownson in

Canton, Massachusetts. With Brownson he studied German, and undoubtedly became imbued with the political radicalism of that ardent reformer. Returning to Harvard, Henry studied the classics and the English poets, and stayed away from social functions. Thoreau always preferred the natural life in the woods of Concord to the scholarly life in the Harvard libraries. "Though bodily I have been a member of Harvard University, heart and soul I have been far away among the scenes of my boyhood."

In his commencement address on August 16, 1837, he discussed the theme that was later to become a dominant aspect of his writing:

> This curious world which we inhabit is more wonderful than it is convenient; more beautiful than it is useful; it is more to be admired and enjoyed than used. The order of things should be somewhat reversed; the seventh should be man's day of toil, wherein to earn his living by the sweat of his brow; and the other six his Sabbath of the affections and the Soul,—in which to range this widespread garden, and drink in the soft influences and sublime revelations of Nature.

Secretly, Thoreau thought he would become a poet.

During his Harvard years he was known to have walked all the way from Concord to Boston to hear Emerson lecture. Finally, a mutual friend introduced the two men, and Henry thus became an informal disciple of the sage of Concord. After his graduation, Henry taught in the Concord school for a few weeks. His tenure, however, was abruptly ended when he refused to beat his students with a rod. On the last day, in a symbolic gesture of contempt toward the stupid ruling, he lined up every student, hit them each once on the hand with the rod, and resigned. He and brother John then decided to open their own school. It was 1837, and with a depression brewing everywhere around them, the two Thoreau brothers first gave classes in their home. Within a short while their school had grown so popular that they shifted it to the then vacant Concord Academy. No beatings were required at the Thoreau school. On the contrary, students were treated to hikes, nature walks, classical poetry, and the gentle mathematical tutoring of John Thoreau. In the meantime, Henry had begun to observe nature in earnest. With spy glass and notebook, he could be seen on his daily walks through the surrounding countryside. The school closed in 1841, leaving Henry back where he had started—jobless and searching for a way in which to be a poet and earn his bread at the same time. The two seemed to him to be mutually exclusive.

He wrote: "If a man has spent all his days about some business, by which he has merely got to be rich, as it is called, *i.e.*, has got much money, many houses and barns and wood-lots, then his life has been a failure, I think."

It was thinking of this sort that led him to decide against any specific profession that would stereotype his life and mold his habits according to socially accepted standards. He needed isolation and nature as other men required money and fame. "I think that I cannot preserve my health and spirits, unless I spend four hours a day at least . . . sauntering through the woods and over the hills and fields, absolutely free from all worldly engagements."

In 1839, however, Thoreau was almost willing to abandon his philosophy in favor of marriage. Pretty Ellen Sewell, a minister's daughter, came to visit her aunt, a boarder at the Thoreau household. When she left, both John and Henry had secretly fallen in love with her. John was the first to propose—and be refused. Henry wrote his offer of marriage in a letter, but Ellen's father, unhappy about the young man's Transcendentalist sentiments, ordered her to refuse him. This romantic interlude did not prevent the brothers from making a boat trip up the Concord and Merrimac rivers, a trip that was to be documented in Henry's first published work, *A Week on the Concord and Merrimac Rivers.* (Published, that is, by himself at his own cost.)

In Concord he hired himself out as a handyman, for he was accomplished at all types of carpentry work, painting, house repair, and the like—but with a book always under his arm. His fellow townsmen resented this somewhat cavalier attitude toward his hard-won Harvard education, and when it became clear that he was happy just to work when it pleased him, they became abusive. To them Henry Thoreau was no more than a loafer.

Ralph Waldo Emerson, however, was impressed by this young practitioner of his own form of Transcendental belief, and he invited Thoreau to live at his home free in exchange for doing chores around the property.

In 1841 Henry settled into the Emerson home in a room at the head of the stairs. Under the guidance of his employer-teacher, Thoreau began to write seriously. He contributed essays and translations to *The Dial* magazine, then coedited by Emerson and Margaret Fuller. He took long walks with his closest friend, Ellery Channing, and conceived the idea of retiring somewhere to write. A farm perhaps or, as he liked to call it, a "garret." At one point he even attempted to buy a farm on credit, but the farmer's wife had second thoughts and convinced her husband to withdraw the offer.

In 1842 his beloved brother John died of lockjaw that had developed from a trivial shaving cut. It was then, too, that Emerson's young son died, leaving both men to comfort each other, and to take solace in the Hindu scriptures they admired so much. Attempting to console himself and his friend, Henry wrote:

> Every blade in the field—every leaf in the forest—lays down its life in its season as beautifully as it was taken up. . . . When we look over the fields are we not saddened because the particular flowers or grasses will wither—for the law of their death is the law of new life. . . . So it is with the human plant. We are partial and selfish when we lament the death of the individual.

Bronson Alcott, the educational reformer, had moved to Concord in 1840, bringing with him his mystical love of nature, his radical school reform methods, and his refusal to pay the poll tax to a slave-holding, war-making government. He spent a good deal of time at the Emerson house, and Henry probably found much to emulate in him. It was, in fact, for refusing to pay his poll tax that Thoreau was jailed three years later, the incident that led to his famous essay, *On Civil Disobedience*.

In 1843, perhaps because of a strained relationship between the two men, Thoreau left Emerson's household to become a tutor in the Staten Island home of Emerson's brother William. The job in New York had a twofold purpose: It provided Henry with a living and made it possible for him to come into contact with Emerson's publishing friends, and perhaps get some of his essays placed. This scheme did prove partially successful, for it was in New York that Thoreau met *Tribune* editor Horace Greeley, who was so impressed with the young man from Concord that he thereafter acted as his unpaid literary agent. Homesickness took hold, however, and after a Thanksgiving visit to Concord, Thoreau packed his few belongings and returned home for good. Now he settled down to helping his father make better pencils and to building a new house for his family.

In August 1844 he and a friend went out to fish. They were frying their catch when a spark caused a fire which quickly spread throughout the forest. Thoreau, already disapproved of by his neighbors, was now reviled as a *dangerous* good-for-nothing. This incident probably helped to seal the growing decision to move off by himself—not as a gesture of defeat, but rather because "To be a philosopher is not merely to have subtle thoughts, nor even to found a school, but so to love wisdom as to live according to its dictates, a life of simplicity, independence, magnanimity, and trust."

To set about fulfilling this ideal of life, he rented a small parcel of land from Emerson in the woods near Walden Pond, and proceeded to build a hut with his own hands. From railroad laborer James Collins's shanty, he acquired a parcel of fine timber.

"Near the end of March, 1845, I borrowed an axe and went down to the woods by Walden Pond, nearest to where I intended to build my house. . . . By the middle of April, for I made no haste in my work, but rather made the most of it, my house was framed and ready for the raising. . . . in the beginning of May, with the help of some of my acquaintances . . . I set up the frame of my house."

Before building a chimney he cooked out of doors. Then when it was all done, he settled down to live, observe nature, and write. To students worrying about earning a living while studying, he recommended that "they should not *play* life, or *study* it merely, while the community supports them at this expensive game, but earnestly *live* it from beginning to end. How could youths better learn to live than by at once trying the experiment of living . . ." of which his own life was the perfect example.

In eight months Thoreau grew enough of his own food to have to spend only $8.74 for extras like corn meal and pork. Ultimately he gave up meat altogether, and before setting out on a trip, he would pray and fast. Furniture in his meditation hut consisted of "a bed, a table, a desk, three chairs [one of which he would place outside as a sign to his friends that he was in the mood for visitors that day], a looking-glass three inches in diameter, a pair of tongs and andirons, a kettle, a skillet, and a frying-pan, a dipper, a wash-bowl, two knives and forks, three plates, one cup, one spoon, a jug for oil, a jug for molasses, and a japanned lamp."

Here in the woods, having pared physical life down to its essentials, Thoreau commenced his search for what the Oriental scriptures had told him was the real Self. He was speaking of the body as the house of the soul when he wrote:

> Before we can adorn our houses with beautiful objects the walls must be stripped, and our lives must be stripped, and beautiful housekeeping and beautiful living be laid for a foundation: now, a taste for the beautiful is most cultivated out of doors, where there is no house and no housekeeper . . . let us first be as simple and well as Nature ourselves, dispel the clouds which hang over our own brows, and take up a little life into our pores.

Thoreau achieved a fine balance between the natural and the intellectual life. His Harvard education and literary tastes prevented him from becoming one of the primitive types with whom he came into contact at Walden Pond, like Alex Therrier, the woodchuck-eating

French Canadian trapper, the Irish railroad workers, or Joe, the Indian guide with whom he toured the Maine woods. In his cabin, Thoreau wrote *A Week on the Concord and Merrimac Rivers* as a memorial to his brother John, in addition to making copious notes (including the Latin genus names for plants and wildlife) for what was to become his best-known book. He was by no means a hermit, but enjoyed the best of both worlds—educated gentleman and Nature's eccentric. He entertained friends, went to town, and tamed the animals around him. Having learned to survey land, he was able to measure the actual depths of Walden Pond. At mealtime he was joined by his pet mouse, who came to trust him well enough to nibble cheese from his hand. Wild birds perched on his shoulders as he hoed his beans and corn and potatoes. Concord farmers driving by in their wagons thought of him as a strange kind of farmer, but not as a recluse.

I did not wish to live what was not life, living is so dear; nor did I wish to practice resignation, unless it was quite necessary. I wanted to live deep and suck out all the marrow of life, to live so sturdily and Spartan-like as to put to rout all that was not life, to cut a broad swath and shave close, to drive life into a corner, and reduce it to its lowest terms, and, if it proved to be mean, why then to get the whole and genuine meanness of it, and publish its meanness to the world; or if it were sublime, to know it by experience, and be able to give a true account of it in my next excursion.

It was easier to set priorities in their proper places, to intuit the purpose of one's existence alone, surrounded only by the seasons and the eerie call of the loon across the water:

> When we are unhurried and wise, we perceive that only great and worthy things have any permanent and absolute existence—that petty fears and petty pleasures are but the shadow of reality. This is always exhilarating and sublime. By closing the eyes and slumbering, and consenting to be deceived by shows, men establish and confirm their daily life of routine and habit everywhere, which still is built on purely illusory foundations.

> I find it wholesome to be alone the greater part of the time. To be in company, even with the best, is soon wearisome and dissipating. I love to be alone. I never found the companion that was so companionable as solitude. . . . A man thinking or working is always alone, let him be where he will.

To a man who so valued the individual soul ("He is blessed who is assured that the animal is dying out in him day by day, and the divine being established"), a government which fostered slavery and had invaded Mexico could not be condoned. In 1846 Thoreau refused to pay his poll tax and was put in the Concord jail when he appeared in town on an errand. One of his aunts learned of his internment and secretly paid the tax, thereby negating his protest. Furious, Thoreau returned to Walden and set down some of his thoughts on the subject for a lecture which was eventually delivered at the Concord Lyceum on January 26, 1848. In the following year Transcendentalist Elizabeth Peabody printed the lecture under the title *On Civil Disobedience* in her short-lived magazine, *Aesthetic Papers*. It was this little-noticed essay that would eventually serve as a key point of reference for civil disobedience movements to come—influencing famous men like Gandhi, Leo Tolstoi, and in our own time Martin Luther King, Jr., and numerous young people opposed, as Thoreau was, to war and racial prejudice.

> It is not desirable to cultivate a respect for the law so much as for the right. . . . The mass of men serve the state thus, not as men mainly, but as machines, with their bodies. They are the standing army, and the militia, jailers, constables. . . . In most cases there is no free exercise whatsoever of the judgment or of the moral sense; but they put themselves on a level with wood and earth and stones; and wooden men can perhaps be manufactured that will serve the purpose as well. . . .

> There will never be a really free and enlightened State until the State comes to recognize the individual with respect as a neighbor; which even would not think it inconsistent with its own repose if a few were to live aloof from it, not meddling with it, nor embraced by it, who fulfilled all the duties of neighbors and fellow men.

It was Thoreau's anarchistic attitude that prevented him from joining the reformers who were advocating similar ideas.

By February 1847, in spite of Emerson's help, he still had had no luck in publishing his first completed book, *A Week on the Concord and Merrimac Rivers.* Frustrated by the poor response of the publishers, Thoreau determined to pay himself for the printing of the book. By September 6, 1847, the experiment in the woods was over; Thoreau sold the hut to Emerson's gardener and left Walden Pond.

I left the woods for as good a reason as I went there. Perhaps it seemed to me that I had several more lives to live, and could not spare any more time for that one. It is remarkable how easily and insensibly we fall into a particular route, and make a beaten track for ourselves. I had not lived there a week before my feet wore a path from my door to the pond side; and though it is five or six years since I trod it, it is still quite distinct. . . . How worn and dusty, then, must be the highways of the world, how deep the ruts of tradition and conformity! I did not wish to take a cabin passage, but rather to go before the mast and on the deck of the world, for there I could best see the moonlight amid the mountains. I do not wish to go below now.

Once again Thoreau moved in with the Emersons, this time to watch over the children while the man of the household was away in England. When Emerson returned in July of 1848, Henry moved back to his parents' home and spent some of his time working in the family pencil factory. His life did not alter much; he walked, wrote, and surveyed land for his fellow townsmen. Later on he was even employed by Concord officials to survey the village boundaries. In 1849, with the money he had earned from his lectures, he paid for the publication of *A Week on the Concord and Merrimac Rivers*. The book was a dismal failure, but that did not stop him from making trips—to Canada and Cape Cod—and writing about those tours as well as writing descriptive essays on the art of walking and a continual barrage of notes in his journals concerning everything from slavery to natural history. When the remaining copies of his unsuccessful book were returned to him, he wrote wryly: "I have now a library of nearly nine hundred volumes, over seven hundred of which I wrote myself. Is it not well that the author should behold the fruits of his labor?"

Perhaps it was this experience that, in the 1840s, drew him farther away from the philosophical tone of *Walden* and closer to the scientific observances of a naturalist.

In 1854 Emerson arranged for the publication of *Walden* for his friend. This book, which sold for one dollar per copy and was serialized in Horace Greeley's *Tribune*, fared much better than the first. But Thoreau remained the private person he chose to be: "I must cultivate privacy. It is very dissipating to be with people too much. . . . I cannot spare my moonlight and my mountains for the best of man I am likely to get in exchange." Ironically, it was the "social" side of Thoreau that brought the public response he had been lacking. When an antislavery address of his was published in *The Liberator*, people suddenly became interested in *Walden* and, later, even in

A Week on the Concord and Merrimac Rivers. When George Curtis, editor of *Putnam's* magazine, asked for his essay on *Cape Cod*, Thoreau agreed. But when Curtis asked him to tone down some of his radical statements regarding religion, he withdrew the piece rather than alter it. Thoreau always practiced what he preached; neither the lure of fame nor wealth nor even friendship could impinge on his principles.

In 1856 John Brown came to Concord. Thoreau found the old man's dedication to the antislavery cause admirable, yet he joined none of the New England groups that were then backing Brown. It was not until the unsuccessful Harper's Ferry raid had passed and John Brown was hanged that Thoreau supported him publicly in a lecture at the town hall. Opinions were conflicting then, and the selectman whose duty it was to announce the meeting refused to do so. Thoreau, with his accumulated antislavery notes under his arm, rang the bell himself. The speech was more in favor of violence in a good cause than for John Brown in particular. Then, just as it seemed that Thoreau the observing individualist was about to turn passionate activist, he went back to minding his own business.

In December of 1860, while at work on a *Kalendar of Concord* and an ecological study of seed dispersion, Thoreau went out to count the rings in some hickory trees. In order to see better, he lay down in the snow, and caught a cold. While only partly recovered, he traveled to Connecticut on a lecture tour and his cold developed into a full-blown case of tuberculosis. The doctor ordered a change of climate, and with Horace Mann, Jr., son of the famous educator, Thoreau headed for Minnesota. There he hoped to observe the Indians, as well as the flora and fauna of the Midwest. But he was really sicker than he thought, and with bushy beard and invalid's gaunt face, he returned home. It was 1862, and Thoreau knew that he would never recover. Calmly he set about ordering his works, putting bits and pieces of manuscript together, and assembling his journals. As one would expect of Henry Thoreau, he continued writing even as he lay sick and dying—observations of nature which resound with the vigor of a man in full health on a fine summer afternoon. He revised his books for publication, for by then he had attained a reputation as a writer and his work was in demand. He dictated letters to his sister, and contributed sketches to *The Atlantic Monthly*. To one of the many visitors who came to comfort him, he said: "When I was a boy, I learned that I must die, so I am not disappointed now; death is as near you as it is to me."

On May 6, a day bright with sunshine, he took a bunch of flowers from a neighbor with thanks, then lay back with his eyes closed and, murmuring "moose" and "Indian," died. Perhaps he was referring to his next incarnation. Thoreau would have chosen with great delight to be born either as a moose or an Indian, just so long as he could be free to roam the woods away from the artificialities of the civilization he railed against. "Not till we are lost, in other words, not till we have lost the world, do we begin to find ourselves, and realize where we are and the infinite extent of our relations." The man who had urged people to cultivate poverty as they would the simple garden herb and thus to make a poem of life died contented in his task.

I learned this, at least, by my experiment; that if one advances confidently in the direction of his dreams, and endeavors to live the life which he has imagined, he will meet with a success unexpected in common hours. He will put some things behind, will pass an invisible boundary; new, universal and more liberal laws will begin to establish themselves around and within him; or the old laws be expanded, and interpreted in his favor in a more liberal sense, and he will live with the license of a higher order of beings. In proportion as he simplifies his life, the laws of the universe will appear less complex, and solitude will not be solitude, nor poverty poverty, nor weakness weakness. If you have built castles in the air, your work need not be lost; that is where they should be. Now put the foundations under them.

Emily Dickinson

I find ecstasy in living—the mere
sense of living is joy enough.

*   *   *

This is my letter to the world,
  That never wrote to me,—
The simple news that Nature told,
  With tender majesty.
Her message is committed
  To hands I cannot see;
For love of her, sweet countrymen,
  Judge tenderly of me!

For twenty-five years Emily Dickinson never left her home. "I do not cross my Father's ground to any House or town." Yet she revolutionized American poetry. She knew few literary people in the limited circle of her acquaintance and published only seven poems (from a collection of nearly eighteen hundred) in her lifetime. Four years after her death, when friends and family collaborated on an edition of her work, poems had to be gathered from scraps of paper, the backs of recipes and envelopes, and hand-sewn bundles hidden in a bedroom desk drawer.

No plausible reason has yet been given for her self-imposed isolation; neighbors blamed it on an unhappy love affair and called her the "nun of Amherst." Current biographers note a mental breakdown caused perhaps by a one-sided love affair with a married man, but the facts of her day-to-day life remain dim.

Emily Elizabeth Dickinson was born in Amherst, Massachusetts, on December 10, 1830, into the home of a prosperous lawyer. Along with her older brother Austin and younger sister Lavinia, she enjoyed a happy childhood surrounded by flowers, pets, and an active village social life. Money was never a problem, and Emily regarded herself as a nonworking gentlewoman. The family were strict, churchgoing Congregationalists who looked askance at the newfangled Transcendentalism that was becoming so popular in Boston, only sixty miles away. Emily's mother remained a shadowy, well-dressed figure throughout the girl's youth. "I never had a mother. I suppose a mother is one to whom you hurry when you are in trouble." It was not until years later, as a helpless invalid, that Mrs. Dickinson made a loving impression on the daughter who tended her night and day.

The town of Amherst was dedicated from its origins to the college located in its center. Emily's grandfather had spent a fortune contributing to the future of the school, whose major function was to produce Orthodox Protestant ministers and missionaries who would spread the Christian message to the far corners of the earth. The townsfolk were largely proud of their college, interested in a certain amount of culture—provided it did not

conflict with their religion—and rather liberal in their
politics. For relaxation they depended on church suppers,
country fairs, and Amherst College Commencement
Teas. After her retirement from the world, Emily would
occasionally appear at these Wednesday teas given by
her father for the faculty and graduating students. One
professor remembered her as sweeping in "clad in im-
maculate white, pass[ing] through the rooms, silently
courtesying and saluting right and left, and sweep[ing]
out again. She seemed more like a spirit than a human
body." This aloofness, adopted sometime during her
mid-twenties, was in direct contrast to Emily's girlhood
personality. Schoolmates remembered her as lively and
mischievous. She was, in fact, voted class wit and was famous for her hilarious parodies of current adult humor
published in the school newspaper. Emily was a bit of a
rebel as a child; she remained unconvinced about salva-
tion and was never able to "give all to Christ"—as town
and school custom required. She preferred to withdraw
into the intricate language puzzles inside her mind and
make poetry instead.

> *I'm nobody! Who are you?*
> *Are you nobody, too?*
> *Then there's a pair of us—don't tell!*
> *They'd banish us, you know.*
>
> *How dreary to be somebody!*
> *How public, like a frog*
> *To tell your name the livelong day*
> *To an admiring bog!*

Her lifelong companions were the flowers in her garden, her sister Lavinia, also a New England spinster, the household animals, and the sights and sounds within a few feet of her Main Street window. She traveled infrequently, once to Washington and once to Philadelphia with her father. Every so often she would stay with cousins near Boston when she was having her eyes treated. It was the trip to Philadelphia, made at the age of twenty-three, that ultimately pushed her into total isolation. There, at the Arch Street Presbyterian Church, she sat enraptured by the fiery sermonizing of forty-year-old Reverend Charles Wadsworth. Admiration was to develop into love, an impossible love on her part, since the minister was already happily married.

> *He put the belt around my life,—*
> *I heard the buckle snap,*
> *And turned away, imperial,*
> *My lifetime folding up*
> *Deliberate, as a duke would do*
> *A kingdom's title-deed,—*
> *Henceforth a dedicated sort,*
> *A member of the cloud.*

Her poetry and letters suggest that this was not the first romantic disappointment of her life. During her school days there had been someone else: a young law student apprenticed to her father, named Ben Newton. This young man had encouraged her as a poet, providing her with the intellectual stimulus that she had been starving for in the midst of what she called the "dimity convictions" of her female companions. She even addressed the liberal, transcendentally inclined lawyer as "Master." But Newton apparently had no idea of the storm he was evoking in his young admirer, for he soon left Amherst and married a woman twelve years his senior. A short while after, at the age of thirty-two, he died of tuberculosis.

> *My life closed twice before its close;*
> *It yet remains to see*
> *If Immortality unveil*
> *A third event to me,*
>
> *So huge, so hopeless to conceive,*
> *As these that twice befell.*
> *Parting is all we know of heaven,*
> *And all we need of hell.*

Having read of her friend's death in a brief newspaper report, Emily wrote to his pastor for information. Her letter of January 13, 1854, characterized Newton as a "gentle, yet grave Preceptor, teaching me what to read, what authors to admire, what was most grand or beautiful in nature, and that sublime lesson, a faith in things unseen, and in a life again, nobler and much more blessed."

Emily Dickinson was indeed a paradox. One part of her could write gay and witty notes to classmates and friends and, in later years, to young nephews and nieces. Even after her break with the world she could still coyly describe herself to an unknown man as "small, like the Wren, and my Hair is bold, like the Chestnut Bur—and my eyes, like the Sherry in the Glass, that the Guest leaves—" Her second self was inclined toward morbidity, a preoccupation with the details of death and dying, and dwelling on the pain of unrequited love. It was this latter side of her that won in the long run; the ghost dressed perpetually in white, guarded by her strange sister Lavinia, who collected cats by the dozen.

Emily's education took her as far as a young, well-bred New England girl could go. The Amherst Academy provided her with a smattering of French and the classics. Here she wrote the lively compositions that made her popular with her classmates. At one point she worked too hard at her studies and fell ill, so that she had to make up a term at the Academy the following summer. Since women of her breeding were not expected to train for any career but that of missionary's wife, or perhaps well-to-do Puritan businessman's wife, Emily was sent on to complete her education at the Mount Holyoke Female Seminary. Here, too, her image was exactly opposite from the eccentric hermit she was to become. She loved school, admired her teachers, and wrote happy letters describing her daily life to her Boston cousins. Although she was assigned Emily Norcross, a dull relative, as roommate, Emily seems to have enjoyed herself. Her reputation as wit and outstanding writer of compositions followed her. Indeed, she even bartered her writing skill for help in mathematics and would exchange compositions for algebra homework.

"Everything is pleasant and happy here. . . . [Head-mistress] Miss Lyon and all the teachers seem to consult our comfort and happiness in everything they do," she wrote to her brother.

Under Miss Lyon, Mount Holyoke was noted for its strict regulations and high standards of scholarship. In addition, the girls were expected to do their own house-keeping chores, even their own cooking, in anticipation of their lifelong domestic functions. Emily was noted for her home-baked bread. (Her father never would eat any-one else's.) Long after her years at Mount Holyoke she continued to cook and bake. By the time she went into seclusion she was also an outstanding gardener who could name flowers with the familiarity of a botanist. Her lovely garden was a famous Amherst attraction. Yet she always hated sewing and cleaning house and managed to avoid those chores, saying, "I prefer pestilence." Lavinia, with the help of a maid, shielded Miss Emily (as she came to be called) from the heavy work around the house.

Emily spent only one year at the Seminary, a valuable and intellectually stimulating year. Courses in geology and botany taught her to observe and record the rhythms of nature minutely. Her poems reflect this sense of ac-curacy but with less concern for science than for the added dimension of fantasy. Here is Emily Dickinson's observa-tion of the hummingbird:

> *A route of evanescence*
> *With a revolving wheel;*
> *A resonance of emerald,*

A rush of cochineal;
And every blossom on the bush
Adjusts its tumbled head,—
The mail from Tunis, probably,
An easy morning's ride.

In the secret of her upstairs room she was creating a new kind of poetry, unheard of in her time. While conventional Victorian poets like John Greenleaf Whittier and William Cullen Bryant were pumping out their perfectly rhymed phrases in praise of nature, Emily Dickinson was creating not only a new and angular way of looking at the world, but also a dissonant and slant-rhymed way of describing it. No wonder that she kept her work a secret. Who in Amherst or even beyond there would allow for her mischievous handling of Biblical phrases and her anti-Puritan puns? The girlish rebel began to give way to the poetic rebel—in secret.

Much unhappiness seems to have been generated by the contemporary religious craze that surrounded her. Mount Holyoke was full of hysterical girls asserting their faith at tearful Sunday prayer meetings. Emily was a private person, she could not "find religion" in a crowd. For months she wrestled with the problem of trying to believe in God, even giving herself up to Miss Lyon's emotional exhortations in His behalf. But her integrity of spirit was too great for her to pretend for the sake of custom, and she sadly dropped out of school for good after a winter vacation at home.

The soul selects her own society,
Then shuts the door;
On her divine majority
Obtrude no more.

Unmoved, she notes the chariot's pausing
At her low gate;
Unmoved, an emperor is kneeling
Upon her mat.

I've known her from an ample nation
Choose one;
Then close the valves of her attention
Like stone.

Nobody at home blamed her for leaving school; she was expected to stay at home until married anyway or, in good New England fashion, to live out the rest of her life there if she remained unmarried. Emily Dickinson continued baking bread, growing flowers, and sending her little flower-accompanied notes of condolence and congratulation to friends and neighbors. Then, after the Philadelphia trip, sometime between 1854 and 1862, she died to the world.

Not with a club the heart is broken,
  Nor with a stone;
A whip, so small you could not see it,
  I've known
To lash the magic creature
  Till it fell,
Yet that whip's name too noble
  Then to tell.

With only a printed edition of Reverend Wadsworth's sermons and his portrait to treasure, Emily retreated into her cave of empty whiteness.

> *A solemn thing it was, I said,*
>   *A woman white to be,*
> *And wear, if God should count*
>   *me fit*
> *Her hallowed mystery.*

> *A timid thing to drop a life*
> *Into the purple well,*
> *Too plummetless that it come back*
>   *Eternity until.*

Reverend Wadsworth continued to correspond with his admiring friend from Amherst—much as Ben Newton might have done for a time. His letters were filled with spiritual comfort and Godly advice, none of which could possibly satisfy the love-starved young woman so far away. Then, in the early spring of 1860, he paid her a visit at home. Emily took one look at his suit of mourning and, breathless with hope, asked him who had died. When she learned that it was his mother and not his wife, she fell back again into despair.

> *Hope is a subtle glutton;*
>   *He feeds upon the fair;*
> *And yet, inspected closely,*
>   *What abstinence is there!*

His is the halcyon table
That never seats but one,
And whatsoever is consumed
The same amounts remain.

To be crossed twice in love was too much to bear. Emily suffered a serious mental collapse which only her writing could overcome. Putting her pain and grief on record, almost like an objective observer watching the habits of a robin, was her consolation. She became fascinated by the mechanics of the mind, of grief, and of the soul's longing for a God who never seemed to appear when needed. Death haunted her continuously, partly under the tempting mask of suicide and partly as the ultimate, intriguing mystery in living. Alone in her room, Emily soldered into poetry her mind's agony together with all the unanswerable religious questions of her childhood.

The brain within its groove
Runs evenly and true;
But let a splinter swerve,
'Twere easier for you
To put the water back
When floods have slit the hills,
And scooped a turnpike for themselves,
And blotted out the mills!

I measure every grief I meet
With analytic eyes;
I wonder if it weighs like mine,
Or has an easier size.

I wonder if they bore it long,
Or did it just begin?
I could not tell the date of mine,
It feels so old a pain.

.   .   .   .

There's grief of want and grief of cold,—
A sort they call 'despair';
There's banishment from native eyes,
In sight of native air.

And though I may not guess the kind
Correctly, yet to me
A piercing comfort it affords
In passing Calvary,
To note the fashions of the cross,
Of those that stand alone,
Still fascinated to presume
That some are like my own.

In 1862 Reverend Wadsworth wrote her that he would be leaving his parish in Philadelphia to settle in California. Now distance would seal the loneliness for good. During the winter of his departure Emily wrote poems continuously in order to fight off madness. Outside her father's comfortable mansion, not so very far away, America, too, was fighting for her sanity. A number of Amherst families suffered the loss of their sons in the Union cause, and it was not uncommon for Emily to find familiar names among the daily newspaper lists of dead and wounded.

I like a look of agony,
Because I know it's true;
Men do not sham convulsion,
Nor simulate a throe.

The eyes glaze once, and that is death.
Impossible to feign
The beads upon the forehead
By homely anguish strung.

Although she kept abreast of town and world affairs through the newspapers and her family, Emily crawled deeper and deeper into her solitude. Between the ages of twenty-four and thirty-one her mind was entirely preoccupied with Wadsworth, her lonely passion for him, and with transcribing the ache into poetry. She became a kind of hermit who alternately rushed to put her poems on scraps of paper and who carefully copied oft-revised work onto notepaper, which she then sewed into booklet form and stored away. She wanted no fame or fanfare and felt betrayed once when her aggressive sister-in-law Sue sent one of her poems without her permission to the local newspaper for publication.

Still, having dedicated her life to poetry, she yearned for an intelligent reading of her work. In April of 1862, on impulse, she wrote to Thomas Wentworth Higginson, minister, abolitionist, and minor literary critic, for an appraisal of thirteen of her poems. Higginson had just written an article of advice to young poets in the *Atlantic Monthly*. Yet all he could do for her was to call her work uncontrolled and recommend that she refrain from publishing. This suited Emily just fine, for it was not publication that she sought but another "Master" like Newton to encourage her in her work. Despite his misunderstanding of this new poetic form, Higginson proved a kindly recipient of her outpourings and their correspondence continued throughout the 1860s. Beyond this mild and relatively useless link with the literary world outside, and a popular poet friend named Helen Hunt Jackson, who urged her to publish, Emily Dickinson was writing into a vacuum while only a few miles distant, the Concord intellectuals flourished.

15 April 1862

Mr. Higginson,

Are you too deeply occupied to say if my Verse is alive?

The Mind is so near itself—it cannot see, distinctly— and I have none to ask—

Should you think it breathed—and had you the leisure to tell me, I should feel quick gratitude—

If I make the mistake—that you dared to tell me— would give me sincerer honor—toward you—

I enclose my name—asking you, if you please—Sir— to tell me what is true?

That you will not betray me—it is needless to ask— since Honor is its own pawn—

In response to Higginson's polite questions about her life and her ideas about poetry, Emily poured out her heart.

25 April 1862

I had a terror—since September—I could tell to none
—and so I sing, as the Boy does by the Burying Ground
—because I am afraid—/ You inquire my Books—/ For
Poets—I have Keats—and Mr. and Mrs. Browning. For
Prose—Mr. Ruskin—Sir Thomas Browne—and the Rev-
elations. I went to school—but in your manner of the
phrase—had no education. When a little Girl, I had a
friend, who taught me Immortality—but venturing too
near, himself—he never returned—/ Soon after, my Tutor, died—and for several years, my Lexicon—was my
only companion—/ Then I found one more—but he was
not contented I be his scholar—so he left the Land.

You ask of my Companions Hills—Sir—and the Sundown—and a Dog—large as myself, that my Father
bought me—/ . . . You speak of Mr. Whitman—/ I never
read his Book—but was told that he was disgraceful—

Her honest emotional accounts of her feelings and her
work as a poet prompted the puzzled Mr. Higginson to
refer to Emily Dickinson as "my half-cracked poetess."
Reserved New England gentlewomen were not supposed
to feel as intensely about literature as she did:

July 1869

If I read a book [and] it makes my whole body so
cold no fire can warm me I know *that* is poetry. If I feel
physically as if the top of my head were taken off, I
know *that* is poetry. These are the only ways I know it.
Is there any other way?

Mr. Higginson visited the red-haired poet at Amherst but he never really understood the value of her work. Helen Hunt Jackson did, however, and convinced Emily to send off some poems—which were not accepted for publication. She even published a novel based largely on Emily Dickinson's life and unrequited love. But the affairs of the outside world gradually began to fade for the shadowy lady in white who fled the company of men and women. By 1870 she had become a consciously determined recluse.

Almost twenty years were to pass before she saw Charles Wadsworth again. He appeared unannounced in 1879 as she worked in her garden. When he left for Philadelphia they resumed their correspondence as though nothing had happened. And Emily never again ventured forth from her home. Her poems about nature, in the form of birds, flowers, and sunsets, took the place of people and love and life . . . even of faith.

Some keep the Sabbath going to church;
I keep it staying at home,
With a bobolink for a chorister,
And an orchard for a dome.

Some keep the Sabbath in surplice;
I just wear my wings,
And instead of tolling the bell for church,
Our little sexton sings.

God preaches,—a noted clergyman,—
And the sermon is never long;

So instead of getting to heaven at last,
I'm going all along!

Her adored father died in 1874, and her mother suffered a paralytic stroke the following year. From 1875 to
1882 Mrs. Dickinson was a helpless invalid under Emily's constant care, while Lavinia, in turn, watched over
Emily. During these lonely and trying years, poetry was
to be what she called her only "playmate." When Wadsworth died at the age of sixty-eight in 1882, Emily
mourned him for the remaining years of her life. Village
people thought of her as "gifted but queer," and friends
and relatives pampered her in her demand for privacy.
Within a year of her mother's and Wadsworth's deaths,
Emily developed Bright's disease but continued to write
nonetheless. In the late afternoon of May 15, 1886, after
having written only the words, "Called back" to her
cousin, she died quietly alone in her room. Publication
of a small part of her output took place in 1890, when
remaining family members, with T. W. Higginson's lukewarm recommendation, presented her poems to the
world.

Perhaps because of her simple and sparse life activity,
Emily Dickinson developed a particularly acute interest
in her own psyche as well as in the minute details of small
town life and nature. She was morbid and extraordinarily
witty at the same time, and she could turn an everyday
object into a foreign treasure with a mere quaint turn of
phrase. For grammar, rhyme, and conscious poetic tech-

nique she had little use. But she succeeded, as had no
American poet before her, in turning grief into poetry.

> *I sing to use the waiting,*
> *My bonnet but to tie,*
> *And shut the door unto my house;*
> *No more to do have I,*
> *Till his best step approaching,*
> *We journey to the day,*
> *And tell each other how we sang*
> *To keep the dark away.*

Walt Whitman

I am the poet of the Body;
And I am the poet of the Soul.

Whitman might also have added that he was the poet of
the ego, and the poet of prophecy as well. He saw himself as akin to the Old Testament prophets in his message to America; he even looked and played the part with
his long white beard, shoulder-length white hair, and
gleaming eyes. Whitman appointed himself American
poet laureate, spokesman for the country's conscience,
representative of the masses. In short, he used himself as
a continued metaphor for both the body and soul of
America.

> *Of all races and eras these States with veins full˜of*
> *poetical stuff most needs poets, and are to have the*
> *greatest and use them the greatest.*
> *Their Presidents shall not be their common referee, so*
> *much as their poets shall.*
>
> *Of these States the poet is the equable man,*
> *Not in him but off from him things are grotesque, ec-*
> *centric, fail of their full returns,*

Nothing out of its place is good, nothing in its place is
bad,

He bestows on every object or quality its fit proportion,
neither more nor less,
He is the arbiter of the diverse, he is the key,
He is the equalizer of his age and land,
He supplies what wants supplying, he checks what
wants checking,
In peace out of him speaks the spirit of peace, large,
rich, thrifty, building populous towns, encouraging
agriculture, arts, commerce, lighting the study of man,
the soul, health, immortality, government,
In war he is the best backer of the war, he fetches artil-
lery as good as the engineer's, he can make every word
he speaks draw blood,
The years straying toward infidelity he withholds by his
steady faith,
He is no arguer, he is judgment, (Nature accepts him
absolutely)

.   .   .   .

He sees eternity in men and women, he does not see
men and women as dreams or dots.
For the great Idea, the idea of perfect and free indi-
viduals,
For that, the bard walks in advance, leader of leaders
The attitude of him cheers up slaves and horrifies foreign despots.

.   .   .   .

Where are you indeed who would talk or sing to America?
Have you studied out the land, its idioms and men?

*Have you learned the physiology, phrenology, politics,
geography, pride, freedom, friendship of the land?
its substratems and objects? . . .*

There was one slight hitch to Whitman proclaiming
himself America's poet: namely, that no one else recognized him as such. Not only did the masses ignore him,
but the literary world would have no part of him either.
Throughout his life the American "laureate's" message
was largely regarded as scurrilous, unpoetic, barbaric drivel.
Nevertheless Whitman not only insisted on printing and
distributing his unrhymed and prosy-sounding verse that
glorified the earthy common man, but he identified with
his subject.

Of pure American breed, large and lusty—age thirty-six
years—never once using medicine—never dressed in
black, always dressed freshly and cleanly in strong
clothes—neck open, shirt-collar flat and broad, countenance tawny transparent red, beard well-mottled with
white, hair like hay after it has been mowed in the fields
—a person singularly beloved and looked toward, especially by young men and the illiterate—one who does
not associate with literary people—never on platforms,
amid the crowds of clergymen or aldermen or professors
—rather down in the bay with fishers in their fishing-
smacks, or riding on a Broadway omnibus, side by side
with the driver, or with a band of loungers over the open
grounds of the country . . . there you have Walt Whitman, the begetter of a new offspring in literature.

So wrote the poet of himself. The newspapers, however, saw him differently:

> The beastliness of the author is set forth in his own description of himself, and we can conceive no better reward than the lash for such a violation of decency as we have before us. . . . The author should be kicked from all decent society as below the level of the brute. There is not wit or method in his disjointed babbling, and it seems to us he must be some escaped lunatic raving in pitiable delirium.

Walter Whitman, Jr., was born in West Hills, Long Island, on May 31, 1819, to a carpenter of English ancestry and a good-natured housewife of Dutch stock. (The poet of Democracy would have been amused no doubt to find that his Long Island home is surrounded today by the stores and theatres of an immense shopping center named in his honor.) The family was large, Walt being the second of nine children, shiftless, and often on the verge of poverty. Walt (he later shortened his name to make it more common-sounding) attended public school, where children were drilled and whipped into learning and where segregation of the races was the rule. The young poet was not much of a scholar and although the family had moved to Brooklyn, Walt preferred to spend time with his crude outdoor Long Island companions—the cattle drivers, farmers, and fishermen. His family's lukewarm Quaker beliefs did not burden him with too much religion, and, except for an occasional sermon by famous Quaker minister Elias Hicks, Walt was not subjected to large doses of morality. That he picked up himself from living contact with nature and observations of simple people and animals in their country habitat.

I celebrate myself, and sing myself,
And what I assume you shall assume,
For every atom belonging to me as good belongs to you.
I loafe and invite my soul,
I lean and loafe at my ease observing a spear of summer
    grass.

. . . .

Stop this day and night with me and you shall possess
    the origin of all poems,
You shall possess the good of the earth and sun, (there
    are millions of suns left,)
You shall no longer take things at second or third hand,
    nor look through the eyes of the dead, nor feed on the
    spectres in books,
You shall not look through my eyes either, nor take
    things from me,
You shall listen to all sides and filter them from your-
    self.

When he was eleven years old, Walt left school to work as an office boy in the law firm of James and Edward Clark. He was given a desk of his own in a corner and a subscription to a circulating library. Edward frequently helped him with his handwriting and compositions. Here the gawky and oversized boy spent his days devouring the circulating library copies of *Arabian Nights* and novels by Sir Walter Scott. The Clarks were kind and even took Walt to church with them on occasion.

In the summer of 1831, while working as a printer's devil for the editor of the *Long Island Patriot,* the boy decided on a career in journalism. He made friends with William Hartshorne, a printer who taught him to set type and who took his part in office squabbles. Thus by the time he was twelve Whitman found himself in the midst of fast-talking newspapermen, politicians, bullies, and local celebrities of every variety. The next year he worked for still another Brooklyn printer and later on for *The Star,* rival to the *Long Island Patriot.* Whitman, the restless wanderer, was to be hired and fired by at least six different papers by the time he was twenty-seven years old.

When Whitman was fifteen his family moved back to Long Island. He was writing for the *Mirror* then and decided to remain in Brooklyn. Physically mature but emotionally adolescent, Whitman spent his youth attending Broadway plays on free press passes, reading novels and poems, and joining debating clubs. In 1835 he moved on to still another printing job and then a year later returned to his family on Long Island to teach school. Walter Whitman, Sr., had different ideas about work and demanded that his son leave off writing and join him as a farm laborer. They quarreled, but Walt continued writing and teaching at nearby Norwich. Teaching in a small country school did not offer as much excitement as the noisy offices of a newspaper, so in 1837 Whitman started his own paper in Huntington. "Then returning to New York city and Brooklyn, work'd on as printer and writer, mostly prose, but an occasional shy at 'poetry.' "

He sold some of his stories to the *Democratic Review*, which also published prominent writers like Poe, Whittier, and Hawthorne. These trivial set pieces were filled with rebellious sons and cruel fathers, and topped always by a strict moral lesson.

Achieving instant success as a magazine writer and becoming editor of a new paper called *The Aurora* prompted the would-be poet to act the role of an important man about town. In his fancy frock coat and beflowered lapel, he boasted publicly about his newspaper. This phase of his life was short-lived, however, for he was soon fired again. The New York scene of the mid-nineteenth century provided him with enough subject matter for a lifetime of poems, and being jobless he had time to devote to his special interests. Ferries, for example, were a passion then:

> I cross'd on the boats, often up in the pilot-houses where I could get a full sweep, absorbing shows, accompaniments, surroundings. What oceanic currents, eddies, underneath—the great tides of humanity also, with ever-shifting movements. Indeed, I have always had a passion for ferries; to me they afford inimitable, streaming, never-failing, living poems.

Another favorite pastime was riding alongside the Broadway omnibus drivers.

How many hours, forenoons and afternoons—how many
exhilarating night-times I have had perhaps June or July,
in cooler air—riding the whole length of Broadway, listening to some yarn . . . or perhaps I declaiming some
stormy passage from Julius Caesar or Richard, (you
could roar as loudly as you chose in that heavy, dense,
uninterrupted street-bass). Yes, I knew all the drivers
then, Broadway Jack, Dressmaker, Balky Bill, George
Storms. . . . They had immense qualities, largely animal
—eating, drinking, women—great personal pride in their
way . . . great studies I found them also. (. . . the influence of those Broadway omnibus jaunts and drivers and
declamations and escapades undoubtedly enter'd into
the gestation of "Leaves of Grass.")

In March of 1846 Whitman became editor of the
Brooklyn Eagle, a four-paged, six-columned paper, which
consisted largely of advertisements. He took his job seriously, though, writing patriotic editorials in favor of the
Mexican War and against the old-fashioned customs of
Europe. America became synonymous for Whitman with
democratic hope for all of mankind—so much so that
he was willing to accept slavery to preserve the Union.

Somehow, even as editor of a circulating newspaper,
Walt continued in his preferred life habits: walking for
a good part of the day, bathing, ferry-riding and theater-
going. To all this his mother used to say: "What will
people think?" And Walt would reply: "Never mind
what they think." This attitude probably contributed
once again to his losing a job, for in 1848 his editorship
at the *Eagle* ended. In February of that year he was of-

fered a job on a New Orleans paper, *The Daily Crescent.*
With a two-hundred-dollar advance and travel expenses
paid, Whitman set off with his fourteen-year-old brother
Jeff on his "leisurely journey and working expedition . . .
through all the middle States, and down the Ohio and
Mississippi rivers."

He kept a diary of this long, tiresome journey by rail,
steamboat, and stagecoach. At last the young patriot
could see first-hand what he had idealized in his imagination: the vastness of America, the raw manners of her
people, and the muddiness of her rivers. Once in New
Orleans, Whitman worked on the *Crescent* from nine in
the morning to eleven at night. Jeff worked near him as
an office boy. It might have been the hours or the hard
treatment of his young brother that created the strained
relations with his new boss. The exact reasons are not
clear but by June 15 Walt and his brother were back in
Brooklyn and jobless.

> . . . plodded back northward, up the Mississippi, and
> around to, and by way of the great lakes, Michigan,
> Huron, and Erie, to Niagara falls and lower Canada,
> finally returning through central New York and down
> the Hudson; traveling altogether probably 8000 miles
> this trip, to and fro.

Now, lying on the beach at Coney Island, he began
experimenting with poetry in earnest. In October he
built a small house for his family on a Myrtle Avenue lot.
The first floor formed a printing office and bookstore,

which Walt's parents tried unsuccessfully to make a profitable business, while the family lived in cramped quarters upstairs. Outwardly Walt was doing nothing; his parents saw him as a hopeless loiterer. But it was during the crucial years from 1850 to 1855 that he was preparing his first book of poems, *Leaves of Grass*.

> *Listen! I will be honest with you,*
> *I do not offer the old smooth prizes, but offer rough new*
>   *prizes,*
> *These are the days that must happen to you:*
> *You shall not heap up what is called riches,*
> *You shall scatter with lavish hand all that you earn or*
>   *achieve,*
> *You but arrive at the city to which you were destin'd,*
>   *you hardly settle yourself to satisfaction before you*
>   *are call'd by an irresistible call to depart,*
> *You shall be treated to the ironical smiles and mockings*
>   *of those who remain behind you.*
>
> . . . .
>
> *You shall not allow the hold of those who spread their*
>   *reach'd hands toward you.*

During this period of incubation as a poet, Whitman befriended a group of young Brooklyn artists. It was fun to mix with "all sorts—young fellows from abroad [who] stopped here in their swoopings: they would tell us of students, studios, the teachers they had just left in Paris, Rome, Florence." In his discussions with these painters Whitman developed the idea that art, rather than conventional standards of behavior, was synonymous with morality. "He who does great deeds, does them from his sensitiveness to moral beauty." Money had no real part in Walt's scheme of things. He was concerned with making his way through what he called the "kosmos," not the practical world, with cultivating his soul, not his pocketbook. Sometimes he worked as a carpenter but most of the time he freely roamed about New York, Brooklyn, and Long Island, taking in the sights, talking to his friends the bus drivers and ferry boatmen. He joined an amateur theater group for a while and attended the opera—preferably the Italian, melodramatic kind. At this point in his career Whitman was accumulating knowledge of everything that came his way: phrenology (study of a man's character from the contour of his skull), history, astronomy, and Egyptology.

"Back to ten thousand years before these States, all nations had, and some yet have, and perhaps always will have, tradition of coming men, great benefactors of divine origin, capable of deeds of might, blessings, poems, enlightenment. From time to time these have arisen, and yet arise and will always arise." The young poet was grooming himself to fill such a place for his time. In 1851 he made a note in a little book he always carried with him: "Be simple and clear.—Be not occult."

Impressed by the doctrines of Transcendentalism, Emerson's in particular, Whitman leaned toward a Pantheistic vision of the universe:

The soul or spirit transmits itself into all matter—into rocks, and can live the life of a rock—into the sea, and can feel itself the sea—into the oak, or other tree—into an animal, and feel itself a horse, a fish, or bird—into the earth—into the motions of the suns and stars.

He began carefully watching his diet and the state of his physical health as well as the state of his soul. From that time on Whitman equated sickness with evil. He was given to meditating alone on the beach at night, gazing at the stars until he felt himself becoming one with the universe, with immortality. Soon even death itself was no longer terrifying.

> *I believe that a leaf of grass is no less than the journey-*
>   *work of the stars,*
> *And the pismire is equally perfect, and a grain of sand,*
>   *and the egg of the wren,*
> *And the tree-toad is a chef-d'œuvre for the highest,*
> *And the running blackberry would adorn the parlors of*
>   *heaven,*
> *And the narrowest hinge in my hand puts to scorn all*
>   *machinery,*
> *And the cow crunching with depress'd head surpasses*
>   *any statue,*
> *And a mouse is miracle enough to stagger sextillions of*
>   *infidels.*

.   .   .   .

> *I hear and behold God in every object, yet understand*
>   *God not in the least,*
> *Nor do I understand who there can be more wonderful*
>   *than myself.*

Such sentiments reflected the influence of the Hindu mystics, in whose works Whitman had read of the eternal nature of the soul, and the unification of all existence through love. In this view of the world Time is virtually abolished in the old sense of past, present, and future. What remains is an eternal Now, surrounded by limitless space where the spirit might travel.

Walt's family continued to resent his way of life, which still consisted mostly of sleeping late, writing for a few hours, and going for long walks. It was in 1854 or early 1855, he later recalled humorously, that "I was working at carpentering and making money when this *Leaves of Grass* . . . came to me. I stopped working and from that time my ruin commenced." The long walks, the lonely meditations at the shore, the talks with his artist and astronomer friends all contributed to the creation of this book of poems. The next step was to get his book published. Undaunted by numerous rejections and with his skill as a printer serving him well, Walt set about printing his poems by himself. How he paid for that first (1855) edition of *Leaves of Grass* remains unknown. At the Cranberry Street printing office of the Rome Brothers, he assisted in the typesetting, proofreading, and, later on, in the distributing of his own book. On July 6 the poems were ready for sale.

WALT WHITMAN'S POEMS, "LEAVES OF GRASS," 1 vol. small quarto, $2 for sale by SWAYNE, No. 210 Fulton St., Brooklyn, and by FOWLER & WELLS, No. 308 Broadway, N.Y.

read the advertisement placed in the *New York Tribune*. But there were no readers eager to hear the voice of this new American bard. Out of one thousand copies, only two or three dozen were sold.

> . . . *Take my leaves America, take them South and take them North,*
> *Make welcome for them everywhere, for they are your own offspring,*
> *Surround them East and West, for they would surround you,*
> *And you precedents, connect lovingly with them for they connect lovingly with you.*

Still nobody "connected." But Walt could not, would not be suppressed. He had discovered within himself the voice of his nation and he was determined to make that voice heard.

> *Walt Whitman, a kosmos, of Manhattan the son,*
> *Turbulent, fleshy, sensual, eating, drinking and breeding,*
> *No sentimentalist, no stander above men and women or apart from them,*
> *No more modest than immodest.*
>
> . . . .
>
> *I believe in the flesh and the appetites,*
> *Seeing, hearing, feeling, are miracles, and each part and tag of me is a miracle.*

In addition to all this exuberant boasting, he added a

preface filled with glorious promise for America. Here he hammered against the outworn European traditions, and urged "the American poets . . . to enclose old and new for America is the race of races." Inevitably the poems were misunderstood by those critics who even bothered to read them. The frank sexual imagery in the poems did not help either. Most readers were offended by his immodesty, chauvinism and obscureness. Poetry then was synonymous with rhyme and with easy-to-follow themes like the beauty of a summer day or bloodless and unearthly love. No wonder these wide, sprawling, unrhymed lines filled with references to the human body and to Walt Whitman, the *typical* nineteenth-century man, proved so offensive.

Whitman was not a shy man; he reviewed his own book anonymously in several newspapers. Each time he tried to give the impression of a wild, new, and uncultivated voice that had sprung up out of the illiterate crowd. He totally ignored the fact of his wide reading and innate refinement. He sent copies of his book to famous literary men and in doing so was surprisingly rewarded. Emerson, on reading *Leaves of Grass*, was so impressed that on July 21, 1855, he uncharacteristically wrote the young poet a warm note glowing with praise:

> Dear Sir:
>   I am not blind to the worth of the wonderful gift of *Leaves of Grass*. I find it the most extraordinary piece of wit and wisdom that America has yet contributed. . . . *I greet you at the beginning of a new career.*

In his own impulsive fashion, Whitman took this as an unqualified endorsement of his efforts. He immediately sent copies of Emerson's letter (which he had reprinted without permission in the *New York Tribune*) to reviewers along with the book. Then in August, 1856, Walt brought out a second edition of *Leaves of Grass*— this one containing his answer to Emerson's letter. Poor Emerson had had no idea of what his gesture would cost him. He was uncomfortable about the whole thing, to say the least.

Bronson Alcott and his friend Henry Thoreau were visiting New York that summer. In his diary Alcott has left a description of his trip to Brooklyn, where he visited with the enthusiastic but unconventional new poet.

Broad shouldered, rouge-fleshed . . . bearded like a satyr, and rank, he wears his man-Bloomer in defiance of everybody, having these as everything else after his own fashion. . . . Red flannel undershirt, open-breasted, exposing his brawny neck; striped calico jacket over this, the collar Byroneal, with coarse cloth overalls buttoned to it; cowhide boots; a heavy round-about with huge outside pockets and buttons to match; and a slouched hat, for house and street alike. Eyes gray, unimaginative, cautious yet sagacious; his voice deep, sharp, tender sometimes and almost melting. When talking will recline upon the couch at length, pillowing his head upon his bended arm, and informing you naively how lazy he is, and slow. Listens well; asks you to repeat what he has failed to catch at once, yet hesitates in speaking often . . . inviting criticisms on himself, on his poems—pronouncing it "pomes."—In fine, an egotist, incapable of omitting, or suffering any one long to omit, noting Walt Whitman in discourse. Swaggy in his walk, burying both hands in his outside pockets. Has never been sick, he says, nor taken medicine, nor sinned; and so is quite innocent of repentence and man's fall. A bachelor, he professes great respect for women.

Another man might have been depressed by the public's indifference to his poetry. Whitman's answer was to bring out still other editions of his poems, each time adding new ones. Once again he called upon the Rome Brothers to print his book, which by 1858 had been enlarged from the original edition to include sixty-eight new and even more controversial poems. Then one February day in 1860 he received a letter from a young publishing firm in Boston asking him to sign with them for a new edition of *Leaves of Grass*. For the first time since he had written the poems he would not have to print them at his own expense. Now with recognition trickling in, Whitman indulged in daydreams of becoming a "wander-teacher," a hobo with a notebook, who would rove across the States spreading his prophecies to the masses. This professional 1860 edition was received with scorn by the reviewers— especially the poems dealing with sex—and the controversy attracted the curious. Nonetheless fate was still against him, for his new publishers were soon forced to declare bankruptcy, and with them went his dreams of success.

Whitman continued to frequent his old haunts, and

in the period between 1860 and 1861 he wrote little. A
new kind of life was preparing itself for him, half night-
mare, half dream. It was to be initiated on April 13, 1861,
when the first shot of the American Civil War was fired
at Fort Sumter. The Secessionists had made their stand;
after the battle of Bull Run, there would be no turning
back.

> *Beat! beat! drums!—Blow! bugles! blow!*
> *Through the windows—through doors—burst like a force*
>   *of ruthless men,*
> *Into the solemn church, and scatter the congregation;*
> *Into the school where the scholar is studying:*
> *Leave not the bridegroom quiet—no happiness must he*
>   *have now with his bride;*
> *Nor the peaceful farmer any peace, plowing his field or*
>   *gathering his grain;*
> *So fierce you whirr and pound, you drums—so shrill you*
>   *bugles blow!*

Whitman was forty-two, too old to be drafted, the
only remaining support for his aging mother, and too independent of mind to undergo army discipline volun-
tarily. His brother George enlisted, while the poet remained in New York as a propagandist for the Union
cause. One day, while searching the newspaper lists of
the wounded, Walt came across the misprinted name of
his brother George. With the fifty dollars representing
his entire savings in his pocket, the poet went immediately to Washington, D.C., to search the army hospitals.

On the trip down, a pickpocket stole the fifty dollars, and Walt arrived at his destination penniless. For two days and nights he looked for his brother. He was on the verge of collapse from hunger and disappointment when he met an old Boston friend named William O'Connor, who had been working in Washington as a government clerk. O'Connor offered Walt a loan and suggested that perhaps George was still with his regiment at Fredericksburg.

Walt went on to Virginia and finally located his brother —who had been only superficially wounded—with the 51st Volunteers in Fredericksburg. Walt stayed with George for a few days, and thus began his new life as army nurse.

> While I was there George still lived in Capt. Francis's tent—there were five of us altogether, to eat, sleep, write, etc., in a space of twelve feet square, but we got along very well. . . . George is about building a place, half hut and half tent, for himself, (he is probably about it this very day,) and then he will be better off, I think. Every captain has a tent, in which he lives, transacts company business, etc., has a cook, (or man of all work,) and in the same tent mess and sleep his lieutenants, and perhaps his first sergeant. They have a kind of fireplace— and the cook's fire is outside on the open ground.

Now no longer safely seated in his patriotic newspaperman's chair in New York, but right in the thick of battle, Walt saw the actual horrors of war beneath the emotional headlines.

. . . the wounded lying on the ground, lucky if their blankets are spread on layers of pine or hemlock twigs, or small leaves. No cots; seldom even a mattress. It is pretty cold. The ground is frozen hard, and there is occasional snow. I go around from one case to another. I do not see that I do much good to these wounded and dying; but I cannot leave them. Once in a while some youngster holds on to me convulsively, and I do what I can for him; at any rate, stop with him and sit near him for hours, if he wishes it.

Walt got so close to battle that he sometimes went out under a truce flag to carry the dead and wounded back to camp.

A sight in camp in the daybreak gray and dim,
As from my tent I emerge so early sleepless,
As slow I walk in the cool fresh air the path near by the
    hospital tent,
Three forms I see on stretchers lying, brought out there
    untended lying,
Over each the blanket spread, ample brownish woolen
    blanket,
Gray and heavy blanket, folding, covering all.

Curious I halt and silent stand,
Then with light fingers I from the face of the nearest
    the first just lift the blanket;
Who are you elderly man so gaunt and grim, with well-
    gray'd hair, and flesh all sunken about the eyes:
Who are you my dear comrade?

Then to the second I step—and who are you my child
    and darling?
Who are you sweet boy with cheeks yet blooming?

Then to the third—a face nor child nor old, very calm,
  as of beautiful yellow-white ivory;
Young man I think I know you—I think this face is the
  face of the Christ himself,
Dead and divine and brother of all, and here again he
  lies.

These first-hand army experiences evoked a huge literary output in the next three years: poetry, essays, newspaper accounts. Shortly before his brother's company pulled out, Whitman returned to Washington with a trainload of wounded men. There he engaged a tiny flat and worked as a copyist in order to keep himself going. Most of his free time he spent in touring the numerous hospitals where the sick and wounded—both Northerners and Southerners—were quartered. He intended to stay for three days and remained for three years.

Daily, with the remains of his tiny income, Whitman brought stamps and fruits and tobacco to the boys in the hospitals. To many dying men the sight of the white-bearded, hearty huge man with the gentle voice represented hope, life.

Oh despairer, here is my neck,
By God, you shall not go down! hang your whole weight
  upon me.

With those men who needed special care, he would often sit all night, or assist in changing dressings, or in helping to clean wounds. Some of the young men grew so attached to him that they would have only Walt and

no one else handle them in their pain. He treated all alike
—Confederate soldiers as well as those on the Union side.

> In my visits to the hospitals I found it was in the simple
> matter of personal presence, and emanating ordinary
> cheer and magnetism, that I succeeded and help'd more
> than by medical nursing, or delicacies, or gifts of money,
> or anything else. During the war I possess'd the perfec-
> tion of physical health. My habit, when practicable, was
> to prepare for starting out on one of those daily or
> nightly tours of from a couple to four or five hours, by
> fortifying myself with previous rest, the bath, clean
> clothes, a good meal, and as cheerful an appearance as
> possible.

The bearded poet soon became a familiar Washington
sight. Nurses, doctors, soldiers, and government officials
came to know him. William O'Connor's circle of friends
welcomed him into their midst. One New Year's Eve he
made a famous whiskey-milk punch that delighted the
literary ladies gathered there. Even President Lincoln got
into the habit of nodding to Walt when they passed on
the street.

> [Lincoln's] face and manner have an expression and are
> inexpressibly sweet. . . . I love the President personally.

Whitman continued writing home, sending dispatches
to New York newspapers and soliciting funds for the
hospitals. Although he sent money home whenever he
could, his mother was never able to make ends meet. She

had a hard enough time managing her mentally ill eldest son and shiftless brood of daughters, in-laws, and grand-children. As usual, Walt could not hope for money from his writing—even those sketches of his war experiences that have come down to us as American Civil War classics. In the year 1864 his only real satisfaction came from his friendships with the young men in the hospitals. A literary friend from the O'Connor circle, John Burroughs, wrote of him then:

> The more I see of Walt, the more I like him. . . . There is nothing more to be said after he gives his views. It is as if Nature herself had spoken. And so kind, sympathetic, charitable, humane, tolerant a man I did not suppose was possible. He loves everything and everybody. I saw a soldier the other day stop on the street and kiss him.

Walt became a kind of big maternal figure beloved by all who met him. His generosity toward the men in the hospitals was doubly great when we consider his own living conditions. On the top floor of a Washington tenement, with his one tin cup, bowl, and spoon, and brown paper serving as a plate for his breakfast of buttered bread, lived the generous philanthropist of the hospital wards. He tried hard to publish a collection of Civil War poems entitled *Drum-Taps* and was waiting constantly for word on the matter from his Boston friends. When one of those friends interceded on his behalf with the Secretary of the Treasury to give the poet a clerkship in his office, the Secretary kept the recommendation letter from Emerson (as a valuable memento, no doubt) but refused to give the "notorious" Whitman a job.

> *Year that trembled and reeled beneath me!*
> *Your summer wind was warm enough, yet the air I*
>   *breathed froze me,*
> *A thick gloom fell through the sunshine and darken'd*
>   *me,*
> *Must I change my triumphant songs? said I to myself,*
> *Must I indeed learn to chant the cold dirges of the baf-*
>   *fled?*
> *And sullen hymns of defeat?*

He might well have been describing his own personal condition as well as the country's when he wrote those lines, for by June of 1864 he had become ill, tired, and homesick. That summer he went home and wrote for the newspapers again in order to earn some money and to spread the truth about the war.

> Whatever pleasant accounts may be in the papers of the North, this is the actual fact [he wrote in *The New York Times* on December 11]. No thorough previous preparation, no system, no foresight, no genius. Always plenty of stores, no doubt, but always miles away; never where they are needed, and never the proper application. Of all the harrowing experiences, none is greater than that of the days following a heavy battle. Scores, hundreds, of the noblest young men on earth, uncomplaining, lie helpless, mangled, faint, alone, and so bleed to death, or die from exhaustion, either actually untouched at all, or

with merely the laying of them down and leaving them, when there ought to be means provided to save them.

Whitman, never a man of the system, exposed the vicious truth of the war as he had exposed the truths of human nature in his poetry. But again few people were willing to listen. Because he could not live on his literary earnings, the poet finally obtained a job in the Department of the Interior through the good offices of his friend William O'Connor. Then just as it seemed he would be able to help his family with their financial troubles, he had to hospitalize his now violently insane brother Jess. This entailed a trip home, and then still another when his brother George was released from a Confederate prison camp. Fortunately Walt was able to pay someone to stay at his job in his absence.

Drum-Taps was still unpublished by 1865; and it was back in Brooklyn, within sight of the print shop perhaps, that he determined once again to print the poems himself. In April of that year his dear President Lincoln was assassinated. Walt viewed the coffin as the President's body lay in state. Someone had placed a sprig of lilacs there and the sight of the flowers stayed with the poet for long after. He was so moved by the tragedy that he added a sequel to *Drum-Taps*, already being printed at the time, a piece entitled "When Lilacs Last in the Dooryard Bloom'd"—one of his greatest poems.

I remember where I was stopping at the time, the season being advanced, there were many lilacs in full bloom.

> By one of those caprices that enter and give tinge to
> events without being at all a part of them, I find myself
> always reminded of the great tragedy of that day by the
> sight and odor of these blossoms. It never fails.

Yet *Drum-Taps* received even worse reviews than had
Leaves of Grass. In *The Nation* young Henry James
(who later regretted having written this review) chas-
tised Whitman for using his hospital experiences in such
a poor cause as his poetry.

> *O I see flashing that this America is only you and me,*
> *Its power, weapons, testimony, are you and me,*
> *Its crimes, lies, thefts, defections, are you and me,*
> *Its Congress is you and me, the officers, capitols, armies,*
> *   ships, are you and me,*
> *Its endless gestations of new States are you and me,*
> *The war, (that war so bloody and grim, the war I will*
> *   henceforth forget), was you and me,*
> *Natural and artificial are you and me,*
> *Freedom, language, poems, employments, are you and*
> *   me,*
> *Past, present, future, are you and me.*
>
> *I dare not shirk any part of myself,*
> *Not any part of America good or bad. . .*

Again, as in the past, Whitman responded by reissuing
Leaves of Grass. In 1866, on a vacation in Brooklyn, he
began re-editing, adding to and changing his poems for
the new edition. He had obtained by then some slight

notoriety in England, for the *Fortnightly Review,* an influential literary paper of the period, had made a point of the American poet's licentiousness. But at least he knew that he was being read abroad.

Winter of 1867 found the "obscene" Walt Whitman living in an unheated room and writing his poems at his desk in the Treasury Building at midnight because that office was warmer than home. The guards liked him and let him in. (Walt always said he got on better with workingmen than with the literary set.) He continued visiting the soldiers in hospitals and paid for a big Christmas dinner at one of them. On February 12, Lincoln's birthday, he received a twenty-five-dollar-a-month raise and moved to a bigger flat. This seems to represent the one big turning point of his career, for it was in 1867 that his cause was taken up by serious literary people in England. A correspondence ensued and a proposed English edition of his poems was agreed upon. Now at last Walt Whitman received recognition as an artist, rather than notoriety as an outcast. Presently he was publishing in a well-known English magazine called *The Galaxy;* soon other British publications were soliciting his work. He received British callers in his poor Washington flat, famous literary critics and young cultivated gentlemen on tour.

Spurred by this new and unexpected acceptance, Whitman decided on a new edition of *Drum-Taps* and still another of *Leaves of Grass.* Even the wealthy and educated people of Rhode Island welcomed him into their midst

on his summer vacation. But Walt, always a social dropout at heart, wrote to his trolley-car conductor friend,
Pete Doyle: "I take a hand in, for a change, I find it en-
tertaining, as I say, for novelty's sake, for a week or two
—but I know very well that would be enough for me. It
is all first-rate, good and smart but too constrained and
bookish for a free old hawk like me."

In February 1869, he befriended the editor of the
Washington Star, who began publishing little pieces by
and about Walt in his paper. This was followed up by a
complimentary piece in the *Chronicle* on the occasion of
the poet's fiftieth birthday. Good fortune never stayed
long in Whitman's corner, for it was at this point, too,
that he was beset by the disabling headaches that marked
oncoming attacks of hypertension and eventual paralysis.
That summer, while on vacation in Brooklyn, Whitman
fell ill. He was still enjoying the praise of English critics
—indeed, Anne Gilchrist, an English literary lady, not
only justified his use of sexual themes and imagery in an
article "from the woman's point of view" but she proceeded to fall in love with him from afar. Whitman was
too preoccupied with personal problems at this time to
take any interest in his English admirer. His notebooks
of the period are filled with references to a harsh psycho-
logical battle with his homosexual feelings toward his
young friend Pete Doyle. Conflicting with this problem
was his strong desire to become a poet-leader for his
country, causing him to work both painstakingly and de-
liberately at becoming a kind of asexual saint.

The idea of personality, that which belongs to each person as himself, or herself, and that you may so heighten your personality by temperance, by a clean and powerful physique, by chastity, by elevating the mind through lofty discussions and meditations and themes, and by self-esteem and divine love, that you can hardly go into a room—or along the street, but an atmosphere of command and fascination shall exhale out of you upon all you meet.

As an ironical postscript to all of this, Mrs. Gilchrist sent him a letter proposing marriage. Of course Whitman rejected it, but not bluntly enough, for the insistent lady continued writing letters in that romantic vein.

On January 23, 1873, Whitman suffered a paralytic seizure from the first of a series of strokes that were to plague him for the rest of his life. Friends cared for him as he lay crippled and alone in his Washington garret. His brother George, married now and settled in Camden, New Jersey, had taken in their mother. He now invited Walt also to come and stay with him. Three days after the poet arrived his mother died. Whitman had always idealized his mother, and elderly ladies in general. The shock of her death soon proved too much for him and he sank into a terrible depression—both mental and physical. Sitting alone within earshot of the rumbling railroad trains, Walt could muse on his faraway Washington friends and on all the dashed hopes of his life.

Poets to come! orators, singers, musicians to come!
Not to-day is to justify me and answer what I am for,

But you, a new brood, native, athletic, continental,
    greater than before known,
Arouse! for you must justify me.

I myself but write one or two indicative words for the
    future,
I but advance a moment only to wheel and hurry back
    in the darkness.

I am a man who, sauntering along without fully stop-
    ping, turns a casual look upon you and then averts his
    face,
Leaving it to you to prove and define it,
Expecting the main things from you.

Yet beneath the self-effacing bravado Whitman con-
cealed his loneliness. In 1874 he acquired a little dog that
followed him everywhere. This might have taken the
edge off his solitude but it did not bring back his health.
Death seemed near, and his work of this period is filled
with allusions to his pact with its heavy shadow.

My hands, my limbs grow nerveless;
My brain feels rock'd, bewilder'd;
Let the old timbers part—I will not part!
I will cling fast to Thee, O God, though the waves buf-
    fet me;
Thee, Thee, at least I know.

Something of the old drive reappeared in 1875 when
Whitman began work on a new edition of his writings to
be published the following year. This surge toward health
was fostered by his rediscovery of nature at the farm of

some friends not far from Camden. The peace and acceptance offered him at the Stafford Farm served to soften
a renewed series of blows from publishers who would not
print *Leaves of Grass* and newspapers that satirized his
eccentric life style, his clothes, and his poetry. He was
sufficiently hurt, however, to seek comfort in the arms of
his English admirers. Sending them a newspaper piece
concerning his lack of acceptance in America (written
by himself), he started an international literary battle
that was to gain him popularity on both sides of the
Atlantic and thus help put him physically back on his
feet.

He liked the Stafford Farm so much that he was soon
spending entire summers out there, bathing in the creek,
singing aloud as he gave himself mud baths, and taking
notes for what was to become a collection called *Speci-
men Days*.

It seems indeed as if peace and nutriment from heaven
subtly filter into me as I slowly hobble down these country lanes and across fields, in the good air—as I sit here
in solitude with nature—open, voiceless, mystic, far removed, yet palpable, eloquent Nature. I merge myself in
the scene, in the perfect day.

As he regained his health, he started to identify himself
with the sturdy trees near the creek, as he had earlier
identified himself with the healthy, animal-spirited bus
drivers and ferrymen.

Now Washington and Boston friends rallied to support

him. In an attempt to heighten his reputation, they engaged lecture halls where he could talk about the death of Lincoln. These lectures eventually became traditional events, given in different cities on the anniversary of Lincoln's death. Wealthy admirers of Walt's poetry occasionally sent gifts or invited him to their country homes. His loyal coterie even arranged for a Western tour when the aging poet was asked to deliver a speech at the Kansas Quarter Centennial Celebration. This was the high spot of his declining years. In his imagination, Whitman had always loved the West and all it stood for. A first-hand view corroborated his notions of its huge, open vistas and its purely American character. To be entirely free of European convention was his goal for his country, and so, it seemed, the goal of the West.

With a Canadian mystic friend, Dr. R. W. Bucke, he toured Canada, Niagara Falls, and northern New York state. Dr. Bucke also at this time conceived the idea of writing Whitman's biography. Although his own desire had been to make his personal life record one with his poems, Whitman was not averse to the formal biography. He even contributed to it himself by writing the first five chapters and by accompanying Dr. Bucke on a pilgrimage to his old West Hills home.

In 1880, twenty-five years after the first edition of *Leaves of Grass*, unscrupulous printers were pirating the poems and publishing them illegally. The poems were popular for their bold sexual subject matter. Whitman never earned a penny from these stolen editions of his book, and the critics continued to be outraged by his "filth." In spite of this, Whitman somehow met with eventual acceptance from the Boston literati. On a lecture tour of New England, he was escorted around historic Concord, wined and dined at the Emersons, and —best of all—offered a contract by a reputable Boston publisher for a new edition of *Leaves of Grass.*

But the dark shadow of rejection always hovered near. On March 1, 1882, the Boston attorney general classified *Leaves of Grass* as obscene literature. The publishers grew frightened, begged Whitman to bowdlerize his poems, and, when he characteristically refused, sent him back his manuscript along with the printer's plates. A nearby Philadelphia publisher sensed the potential advantages in the publicity of the affair and promptly signed him on. For a while the poems sold well precisely because they had been "banned in Boston." But the sale soon dwindled down to nothing and Walt was back where he started.

In 1884, alone in a shabby house on Mickle Street in Camden, the "good gray poet" lived out his days among heaps of papers and manuscripts. A housekeeper, with her menagerie of birds, dog and cat, cared for his needs and got in his way. His paralysis and lameness grew worse. People recall seeing him hobbling down the street hawking his own books from a basket he carried on his arm. Sometimes he would go down to a tavern by the river and drink beer with the ruffian-type friends he had always loved so much. Neighbors gossiped about his habits as much in these declining years as they had when he was young. Now no more than a bad old man to the outside world, Whitman became something of a living legend to his loyal friends, both English and American. Great poets and famous literary figures came to see him in his poor little house on Mickle Street. Some even went so far as to pool their money and buy him a buggy. A young sculptor and a famous portrait painter simultaneously worked on representations of this suddenly most photographed American poet. Banquets were given in his honor. Then in 1888, with real recognition pouring in on him and good friends always available with money and assistance, he suffered another stroke. A male nurse, paid for by friends, was in constant attendance. A young man named Horace Traubel ran errands, copied his conversations word for word, and was even married in Whitman's tiny room.

From the time he was stricken, Whitman set about clearing up his earthly affairs. He made out a will, reorganized his poems, and even selected his own tomb. The latter days were spent in dictating *Good-Bye, My Fancy*, a miscellany on death, to Horace Traubel. There was no sadness on Whitman's part, only acceptance and a continued belief in poetry as religion.

> As in a swoon, one instant,
> Another sun, ineffable, full-dazzles me,
> And all the orbs I knew—and brighter, unknown orbs;
> One instant of the future land, Heaven's land.

He died quietly on March 26, 1892—waiting, he had

said, for the summer. For the first time, the newspapers gave large amounts of space to Walt Whitman. Critics asked rhetorically if he would be remembered in a hundred years. The controversial nature of his poetry was discussed for the millionth time; and multitudes attended his funeral. It was an ironic recognition, this last one. But Walt Whitman would have well understood it, as he well understood his America.

These States are the amplest poem,
Here is not merely a nation but a teeming Nation of
  nations,
Here the doings of men correspond with the broadcast
  doings of day and night,
Here is what moves in magnificent masses careless of
  particulars,
Here are the roughs, beards, friendliness, combativeness
  the soul loves,
Here the flowing trains, here the crowds, equality, di-
  versity, the soul loves.

The Brook Farm Commune

> How many dreamers! How many dreams realized!
> How many dreams expired in its expiration. It was
> not lost—not all. It was the greatest, noblest, brav-
> est dream of New England.
>
> ISAAC HECKER

"Utopians with artistic, technical, professional skills;
with children of nine and up, join our homestead-school-
community now forming as home base to develop experimental village for inner city poor. No salary. Subsistence
communal responsibility. . . ." On July 4, 1970, 123 years
after the total failure of Brook Farm, the preceding an-
nouncement was made in the Personals Column of a
prominent national political magazine. It is one of many,
for despite its failures the communal impulse is far from
extinguished in America. As long as there are idealists,
dreamers, political reformers, off-beat religious and food
cultists, there will be communal farms. Brook Farm was
not the first nor will it be the last great socialist experiment in America.

Today from the hills of New England to the mesas of

Colorado and the forests of the Northwest, communes abound. There is even a kind of underground Farmer's Almanac catalog in print which provides advice on everything from planting tomatoes to survival in the wilderness and the art of water-distilling. By comparison with the first band of intrepid reformers who accompanied George and Sophia Ripley in their wagons to Brook Farm on April 12, 1841, even the most impoverished and idealistic twentieth-century commune is ten steps ahead. The reasons motivating such groups, however, remain essentially the same. As Nathaniel Hawthorne, one of the earliest members, put it: "Brotherhood."

The Brook Farm experiment putting brotherhood into action began really with the economic depression of 1837. Concerned New Englanders like George Ripley, Theodore Parker, and Ralph Waldo Emerson, who had lost their faith in business and businessmen, recognized that the insecurity of the workingman called for a new social system. Utopian Socialism was a popular philosophy of the time, and the ideas of men like Robert Owen and Charles Fourier were heatedly discussed both in print and in the Boston lecture halls. Simultaneously the Transcendentalist movement had emerged as a reaction to the conservative Unitarian and Trinitarian Puritanism of New England. Under the guidance of men like Emerson, these Transcendentalists rejected the doctrine of divine revelation in favor of the self-sufficiency of the human mind. Nature, as Emerson wrote, was "An Apparition of God," and man's goal was to realize the Over-Soul in his own life by refusing to distinguish between the divine and the natural.

A new and passionate interest in man's real and material life as opposed to the church's promises of revelation characterized these Transcendental reformers, particularly as it applied to the lot of the workingman. On September 19, 1837, the Transcendentalist Club was born. Purporting to deal with social issues and guided by the philosophy that intuitional knowledge was superior to that of the senses, the group met informally, taking no records, electing no chairman, and opening its doors to all. Men like Dr. William Ellery Channing, a reformer as well as a minister, orated brilliantly at these meetings and succeeded in charging the minds of younger men like George Ripley. Theodore Parker, another impressive preacher and social reformer, talked also of creating the ideal community which, as Channing had said, was one "where labor and culture should be united."

The idea for Brook Farm began here, taking root in the mind of the thirty-five-year-old Ripley, a Unitarian minister who had graduated first in his Harvard class of 1823.

By the fall of 1839 he had become business manager of *The Dial* magazine, with Margaret Fuller, "the most learned woman in America," acting as editor. The magazine served as a forum for Transcendentalist thinkers like Emerson, Parker, and Channing. George Ripley became so actively involved in the new movement that it soon became impossible for him to continue preaching traditional Unitarian sermons. In May of 1840 he resigned from his parish and took his wife, Sophia Willard Dana, to spend the summer on the farm of Charles Ellis, a wealthy friend in West Roxbury, Massachusetts. Here, in direct contact with nature (he milked cows and did some gardening), Ripley conceived of a new form of life. Taking long walks and talking with his friend Theodore Parker (who dared to preach Transcendental philosophy from his own Roxbury pulpit), Ripley strengthened in his resolve.

Back in Boston at the Elizabeth Peabody bookshop on West Street—a gathering place for these intellectual and theological idealists—Ripley propounded his scheme for an experimental commune. Ripley hoped less to make any great revolutionary change than to reform men by setting an example on a small scale. He was not ardently antislavery, nor was he passionately in favor of women's rights. His goal was to make a modest copy of Robert Owen's already successful commune in Scotland. In 1840 when Ripley was planning for his socialist experiment there were already thirty or forty other such communities in the making—not to speak of the already existing groups of Shakers and Quakers, the religious-minded communes having well preceded the social ones.

Without taking into account the inadequate, gravelly soil of his friend Ellis's farm, Ripley persuaded his hosts of the previous summer to give him their place on a long-term, rent-free lease for the experiment. A little fresh brook flowed past the farmhouse, providing the place with its name. Ripley, Parker, Orestes Brownson—all Transcendentalist ministers eager to reform the conditions of mankind—joined together in the idea. But Emerson, the guiding light behind the entire movement, stubbornly refused to join. He remained unconvinced that communal living would be the answer to society's ills. Moreover, as the experiment developed, he not only dissociated himself from it but started to criticize it and poke fun at it as well. "A perpetual picnic," he was later to call it.

George and Sophia Ripley were disappointed when Emerson and then Margaret Fuller both refused to join Brook Farm. But on April 2, 1841, the Ripleys, George's sister, and fifteen others drove the nine miles from Boston to West Roxbury and Brook Farm. Without making any formal arrangement, without settling the terms of the eventual purchase, unaware of the condition of the farm, they moved in. Fortunately William Brockway Allen, a young New Hampshire farmer, was one of their company. He was, in fact, the only member of the party with any farm experience at all. And except for Ellen Barker, a domestic, and Minot Pratt, a printer, the other well-bred, college-educated communards could do little in the face of what they found there. The Ellises had left the place in a mess. As printer of Ripley's articles, Mr. Pratt had become indoctrinated with Transcendental socialism. He and his wife were "faithful and fervent workers"—and they soon made the farm livable.

On April 12 writer Nathaniel Hawthorne invested one

thousand dollars in two shares of Brook Farm and joined the community. Engaged to Sophia Peabody (Elizabeth's sister), he hoped to earn enough from his investment to afford to marry. Under the influence of Ripley's great optimism, he pictured himself building a lovely house for his future wife and thus set eagerly to work pitching hay, forking manure, and caring for the pigs. In 1852 he published *The Blithedale Romance*, a tale based on his Brook Farm experience—which had turned sour within a week of his arrival.

"On the whole, it was a society such as has seldom met together; [he writes in his novel] nor, perhaps could it reasonably be expected to hold together long. . . . We were of all creeds and opinions, and generally tolerant of all, on every imaginable subject. Our bond, it seems to me, was not affirmative, but negative. We had individually found one thing or another to quarrel with in our past life, and were pretty well agreed as to the inexpediency of lumbering along with the old system any further. . . . My hope was, that, between theory and practice, a true and available mode of light might be struck out; and that, even should we ultimately fail, the months or years spent in the trial would not have been wasted, either as regarded passing enjoyment, or the experience which makes men wise."

In his personal diary Hawthorne was less tolerant and complained bitterly of exchanging his pen for a pitch-fork. Of the more enthusiastic farmers he wrote: "New enthusiasm grew as flimsy and flaccid as the proselyte's moistened shirt collar after a quarter of an hour's labor under the July sun." But, for the time being, Hawthorne—with grumpy countenance—remained.

Although the fate of Brook Farm became inextricably tied to the lives and fortunes of George and Sophia Ripley, they kept no formal records. Except for letters to friends and later Ripley's magazine articles, no personal progress report remains. Interestingly, a letter from William Brockway Allen, the uneducated farm hand, to his New Hampshire sweetheart, in May of 1841, provides a very real and living portrait of Brook Farm life in its early days.

He wrote: "There are about two hundred acres of land including mowing, pasturing, tillage, and wood land. . . . It is beautifully diversified with hills and valleys there is a large meadow on it which is partially surrounded with hills, some of which are covered with shrubs and trees, others are cultivated with various crops, others are occupied as a pasture for the cows. . . . The house is a large two-story one, painted white with green blinds, standing on the rising ground overlooking the meadow and babling brook as it winds its way towards the River. There are four rooms on the lower floor of the house, connected with the main house is a back kitchen, workhouse, Chaise house, etc. We have a very large barn with a cellar to it opening on the south East side, this is occupied principly as a stable for the Cows, Oxen, Horses, Pigs &c. We have at present nine cows two oxen two Horses and four pigs. . . .

"I will first inform you how we spend a day in the first

place. Mr. Farley and I rise about 4 o'clock and make two fires one in the kitchen and the other in the parlor, Farley then blows a horn at a quarter before 5, all hands then turn out to milk and take care of the cattle and Horses and pigs while the rest milk. All things being put to order at the barn we return to the Woodshed and pull off our boots frocks &c, and prepare for breakfast which is ready at half past 6 o'clock, after breakfast we talk a while and then prepare for the labours of the forenoon by putting on our coarse boots, blue frocks &c. We then proceed to carting manure or such work as is to be done. The way these literary characters appear in a barnyard shoveling is a perfect caution to all labouring men. We work till about ½ past 11 o'clock then all hands turn out put up the team and feed the cows pigs &c. and prepare for dinner which is served up in fine stile at ½ past 12 o'clock. We eat and talk then talk and eat till we get enough, then we retire to the parlor or to our rooms as we please till 2 o'clock, then all hands are summoned to the fork, the shovel, hoe or spade as the case may be, the afternoon passes in all respects like the fore part of the day, we quit work in the field about 5 o'clock so as to get through with our work at the barn by sundown, the process of feeding Cows, Milking &c. is the same at night as in the morning. Thus passes a day, or that is the way we spend a fair day, rainy days are somewhat different though the milking &c. goes on as usual, but after breakfast all go to their studies if they choose, sometimes I read and sometimes I go to work just as I happen to feel....

"One dollar is what they allow for every ten hours work done by any person either man or woman but there shall be but ten hours work paid for in one day. Each person is to choose his or her own employment as far as is practicable and all receive the same price for their labours. No charge shall be made for the board or schooling of any child under 12 years of age. These are some of the general ideas of this community but it is not established yet but they hope to get it organized this [Summer]."

Elizabeth Peabody solicited funds for their cause, and in a short time a Brook Farm School was established in a small house across the road from the "Hive"—as the main house was called. More joined the community, and by midsummer George Ripley claimed: "We are now in full operation as a family of workers, teachers, and students."

The young men wore tasseled caps and rough brown farm tunics belted at the waist, while the girls wore muslin dresses with flowers or ribbons and, in defiance of current modest fashion, left their hair flowing loose. Non-Brook Farmers were condescendingly referred to as *civilisees*.

Free time, what little there was of it, was filled with dancing, self-consciously intellectual conversations filled with puns, picnics on Cow Island or in their Piney Wood, outdoor banquets and masquerades, Shakespeare readings, and, in winter, skating on the nearby Charles River.

Meals were served in the Hive and consisted of simple food gathered from the farm. The members gathered family-style on white-painted benches around the long tables in the low-ceilinged dining room. The dishes, too, were all white, unadorned, with mugs instead of cups and saucers for milk, tea, or coffee. White linen tablecloths covered the tables—one of which was reserved specifically for vegetarians and people who followed other food cults. Younger boys served as waiters; George Ripley sat at the head of the table with Sophia at one side and his sister, Miss Ripley, dispensing coffee and tea at the other. Prayers were never held at table, the farmers having become free-thinkers and communards first and believers second. Visitors were welcomed, and guests like Emerson, Margaret Fuller, and Bronson Alcott came by to share dinner and stimulating conversation.

Soon they were taking in more members, some, like Almira Barlow, on a boarder basis. Almira was a recently deserted wife, a great beauty, and the mother of three boys. Her flirtations proved a delight to the men and a horror to the women, who washed and scrubbed and ironed while she played.

Charles Dana, a young cousin of Sophia Ripley's and a recent Harvard graduate, arrived and was highly regarded thereafter as both a scholar and griddle cake server.

The organization of work soon came under three major headings: The Field, The Mechanical, The Domestic. Each group was then further divided into smaller units, always of an uneven number so as to make voting possible. The Field workers cared for planting, hoeing, weeding. The Mechanics handled carpentry, printing, shoemaking, and chinaware production. Domestic units busied themselves with the dormitory, consistory, kitchen, washing, ironing, mending. Men lent a willing hand in these tasks. In fact, young men rather enjoyed helping the girls in the kitchen, as it afforded them a chance to socialize. Despite Sophia Ripley's unimpeachable reputation for modesty and her strict control, Bostonians found the mixture of boys and girls together a daring and unwise experiment. Still the worst that is recorded to have happened there is the marriage proposal by one of the young men to his sweetheart as they washed and dried the dinner dishes.

Students at the school paid off part of their tuition by helping with chores. Not surprisingly, despite the fact that even the most scholarly Brook Farmers took pleasure in their menial tasks, the school soon became the only real immediate source of income. Food produced was quickly consumed at home, leaving little or no surplus to market. The gravelly soil proved unfit for crop-growing on a large scale and required doubly back-breaking labor. But subscribers kept coming. Working conditions in the outside world were probably still harder in those early years of 1841 to 1843.

Each subscriber to the Farm was entitled to the tuition of one pupil for every share of stock held. Twelve months' notice given to the trustees was required before stock could be withdrawn. Then the subscribers could withdraw their stock with interest. Two months' probation time was required of every potential resident, after which a two-thirds membership vote determined his acceptance.

Labor offset the price of board. Three hundred days' labor equalled a year and entitled the associate to one share of the annual dividend. From May to October sixty hours of work comprised one week and from November to April forty-eight hours. Boarders like Mrs. Barlow paid four dollars per week for rent, fuel, light, and washing. Members with working children over ten were charged half the regular rate; those with children under ten paid three dollars and fifty cents for each child—"exclusive of washing and separate fire." The Farm was established as a joint stock company in which all members voted and owned shares.

The Hive contained rooms where children were left in the care of Nursery Groups while their mothers worked —antedating the Day Care Center concept by a century. Additional buildings included the Eyrie, containing the school house and the Ripleys' quarters with their famous library of foreign- and English-language books; the Cottage, containing schoolrooms for younger children and said to be the prettiest building; and Pilgrim House, used for laundry and tailoring rooms and later a print shop. A horse-rake and seed drill were the only modern implements used. Oxen and manual labor provided the rest. Lumber could not be bought in large quantities, and the nine miles separating the farm from the central market kept two men in wagons constantly on the roads, making two less in labor.

Despite these and many other difficulties, visitors and neighboring farmers smiled at the sight of elegant women doing scullery work while their scholarly men hoed potatoes and cleaned stables. Teachers frequently left off hoeing to meet their pupils; but pupils did not always return the compliment. Only one or two rooms boasted curtains or carpets—most were Spartan and bare. The Hive provided them with a discussion hall on rainy days; and while the young people scattered themselves on the stairs and floors, everyone joined in on the pros and cons of subjects like: "Is labor in itself ideal, or, being unattractive in character, do we, in effect, clothe it with the spirit we bring to it?" In spite of such long-winded titles, little in-depth intellectual work was accomplished there— as Hawthorne sadly learned. But there was much in the way of stimulating new ideas, and especially radical ones. Young people were instilled with a passion for intellectual work and a sense of responsibility to the community. Study hours were unfixed; the pupil would have to make his or her own time.

The Infant School provided for children under six and was in the care of educated women like Amelia Russell and English-born governess Georgiana Bruce. Children under ten attended primary school, where Sophia Ripley's language classes were most popular. The Preparatory School, which fitted students for college in six years, became so well respected that Harvard authorities recommended it to their prospective students. After all, George Ripley, its headmaster, had been the first scholar of Harvard's graduating class of '23.

Young people came to the Brook Farm school from as

far away as Florida and Manila. Charles Dana taught Greek and German. George P. Bradford, "a great teacher, who aroused in his pupils a love of learning and a deep attachment to himself," headed the Department of Belles Lettres. George Ripley taught math, his niece taught drawing, and John Dwight, also a Harvard-educated ex-minister and Transcendentalist, taught music and Latin. Each pupil was required to take the course in agriculture and to perform at least two hours of manual labor a day.

Men and women were equal and shared responsibility of all kinds. Few married couples lived there and, although there was local gossip, no scandals emerged as a result of the Farmers' liberal views. Homer Doucet, a physician who stayed from 1844 to 1846 (the period of the Farm's decline), wrote: "I never heard loud or boisterous language used; I never heard an oath; I never saw or heard of anyone quarreling; I never knew that anyone was ever accused or suspected of having acted in an ungentlemanly or unladylike manner anywhere on the place."

Perhaps George Ripley's optimism, his courtesy and perpetual good temper in the face of all odds set the prime example for all. Well anticipating future American nonconformists and providing a model for the others, he let his beard and hair grow long. The girls wore short skirts over bloomers, the symbol of emancipated womanhood. Mrs. Ripley, although she later devoted more time to the school, was a cheerful, refined lady who shocked her well-bred *civilisee* friends by working ten hours a day on the laundry. Most of the educated male members were ex-clergymen who had left their pulpits because the principles of their church had proven too conservative for them. They wanted paradise now—and here. No wonder that literary critics would later claim that for Hawthorne, at least, the entire Brook Farm experience was something apart from his real life, unrelated to the nature of the man, no more than a passing dream.

"The real me," he wrote, ". . . was never an associate of the Community. There has been a spectral appearance there, sounding the horn at daybreak and milking the cows and hoeing the potatoes and raising the hay, toiling in the sun and doing me the honor to assume my name. But the spectre was not myself."

Like a bad omen, Hawthorne's increasingly negative mood was to foreshadow the final decline of Brook Farm. He was seen as the exception to the rule, however, when on October 11, 1841, in high spirits, Brook Farm was bought from the Ellises by the shareholders for ten thousand five hundred dollars. Two weeks later, on October 27, Hawthorne left the commune.

Although the harvest was scanty that fall there was much music and dancing. Emerson, in the meantime, had nothing but unkind words for his Transcendentalist friends. He derided their scheme as "a French Revolution in small; and an Age of Reason in a patty-pan." Emerson rankled at the thought that one man could be hoeing while another looked out the window and that both still received the same pay.

In February of 1842 the Articles of Association were put to paper. There were to be twelve directors: three for Industry, three for Education, three for Finance, and three for General Direction. A Board of Trustees was composed of the six latter members. Brook Farm seemed to be on its way at last. But, as in every Eden, a snake, here in the form of Fourierism, lurked among the trees.

Charles Fourier was an eccentric French social philosopher who believed that the only form of labor should be that which is harmonious and pleasurable to the individual. He dreamed of a system of what he called Phalanxes—small socialistic units of shared labor with life centering in an immense hotel-like structure. Here where men would constantly keep changing from task to task—at their own discretion and when the spirit moved them—perfect individual liberty would be achieved. Work would be not only rewarding but absolutely pleasurable. Elected officials, voted into office by Harmonious Groups of workers who were divided and subdivided into units, would supervise this Utopia. Fourier also believed in free love and that the oceans of the world would gradually turn into a kind of cosmic lemonade!

Although this philosopher had already died by 1842, he had left an ardent disciple in the person of one Albert Brisbane, an American who returned to the States to introduce these ideas in Horace Greeley's *New York Weekly Tribune*. George Ripley, like many other intelligent, well-intentioned men of his time, read Brisbane's exciting promises of luxurious Phalanxes taking over the country at a mere thousand dollars a share. He painted pictures of huge hotel-style suites, rooms, and porches for sunbathing—a veritable Acapulco for the common man. What he neglected to state was that not one such Phalanx had ever existed outside his own imagination. Nevertheless Fourier fever began to take hold.

In the spring of 1842 the Brook Farmers received so many applicants that they built the Eyrie in only a matter of weeks in order to accommodate them. Used for concerts because of its superior acoustics, the building was long and narrow, made of gray-painted wood, with high French windows facing onto a group of terraces that descended toward the brook.

When young William Brockway Allen finally did marry, he left Brook Farm to settle in New Hampshire. The intellectual and social climate had proven too much for this simple farm boy. Less quietly and more comfortably from his vantage point at Concord, Emerson continued to send a barrage of pointed arrows at George Ripley's band of reformers: "Those who are urging with the most ardor what are called the greatest benefits of mankind, are narrow, self-pleasing, conceited men; and affect us as the insane do. They bite us and we run mad also. . . . It is a buzz in the ear."

For his part, George Ripley kept the faith in good times and in bad. In a letter to the *New York Tribune* on August 8, 1842, he boasted of the Farm's success:

We number now about seventy souls, of whom some
fifteen are Associates, the remainder pupils, boarders,
and persons whose labor we are obliged to hire. We own
two finished houses, hire another, and are building two
more. As soon as these are done we shall have not less
than one hundred persons. . . . A shoemaker, a black-
smith, and a carpenter would serve us greatly, and keep
within ourselves large sums which we now have to pay
out. We congratulate ourselves especially that our organization is not fixed and finished but constantly tending toward something better.

Dial editor Margaret Fuller came for a visit, descend-
ing on Brook Farm like a haughty princess come to grace
the masses with her presence. She was an important intellectual figure of her time, a tall, imposing, unattractive woman, whose aggressive and domineering habits
did not endear her to many. Miss Fuller was later to
become a journalist for Horace Greeley's *Tribune* and a
fighter for Italian independence. In 1842, however, she
was still holding court with Emerson in New England;
and when she did not get the unbounded attention she
desired at Brook Farm, she made a point of sleeping late,
sending the worshipful Georgiana Bruce for her morning
coffee, and making comments on the rudeness and "want
of conventional refinement" prevalent there. What Miss
Fuller did not wish to accept was the fact that newcom-
ers frequently went unnoticed "to convey the lesson at
once of the unimportance of one individual more or less
in the community."

On October 17, 1842, Hawthorne could contain his

dissatisfaction no longer and, in a letter to Secretary-
Treasurer Charles Dana, gave notice of his withdrawal
from the Community.

> I ought, some time ago, to have tendered my resignation
> as an Associate of the Brook Farm Institute, but I have
> been unwilling to feel myself utterly disconnected with
> you. As I can see but little prospect, however, of return-
> ing to you, it becomes proper for me now to take the
> final step. But no longer a brother of your band, I shall
> always take the warmest interest in your progress, and I
> shall heartily rejoice at your success—of which I can see
> no reasonable doubt.

He was joined in leaving by other old friends like William Allen and Orestes Brownson. But this small exodus
did not stop the enthusiasm of the other inhabitants,
who continued to welcome new applicants almost daily.
One of these was Isaac Hecker of New York, a mystic
and a baker. He had come to the Farm to get away from
family pressure at home and to seek the solitude in nature
that might afford him a clue to certain spiritual visions
that had been occupying his mind of late. Certain fellow
Brook Farmers regarded the strange young man as "moon-
struck." Others, like the indefatigable Brook Farm vamp,
Almira Barlow, found him mysterious—but charming.
On January 19, 1843, in a letter to his family, Hecker
wrote of his new experience:

> The bread-baking has fallen into my hands. I take
> whole charge of the bread for the Community, in which

there are ninety persons, consuming about fifty to
sixty lbs. of bread a day, which I bake in one batch once
a day. They have had very poor bread. . . . The room
that I now have is in the same house with the oven,
which my former room was not . . . and all things are
comfortable. When I am not at the bread I sit in my
room; that is in the daytime. . . . In the evenings there
is always something taking place. I have this evening
been to a Singing School of which there are two; the
first has been these four months; the second commenced
last week for new beginners. . . . Taught by Mr. Dwight
of the Community—a lecture of his will be in the next
Democratic Review for February, on Handel's *Messiah.*
. . . Last evening, Mr. Alcott and Mr. Lane . . . were
here, and there was a "Conversation" held in the parlor
of the house called the Eyrie. . . . Every evening is occupied with a meeting and sometimes two.

Hecker brought with him the unearthly glow of mysticism. Brook Farm already had one resident mystic in
Charles Newcomb, a strange, effeminate-looking youth
from Rhode Island, whose poetry promised a genius that
never emerged and who hung wooden crucifixes and por-
traits of the Virgin in his room along with a photo of a
famous female dancer of the period. Newcomb could be
heard through the thin walls at night—reciting a litany
of Greek and Latin verse or praying loudly.

The mystical impulse spread like wildfire and even
Mrs. Ripley herself did not remain unaffected by the
new surge of religious feeling that struck the Farm in 1843.
She became imbued then with the faith that would later

in life turn her toward the Catholic Church as a convert. Almira Barlow, on the other hand, was not much interested in religion. She occupied her time in trying to seduce the celibate Mr. Hecker. On May 27, because of her continued "activities," Mrs. Barlow was voted out of Brook Farm by a majority decision. She somehow managed to obtain a reprieve (due to her flirtatious influence with members of the governing board, no doubt) and remained to torment poor young Hecker. Apparently withstanding her temptations became too great a trial for the mystic, for he left Brook Farm to join Bronson Alcott and Charles Lane at "Fruitlands"—an even more Spartan community, which prohibited the eating of any animal product whatsoever, and the drinking of tea or coffee. This was the first stage of Hecker's ultimate conversion to the Catholic Church, his later entry into the priesthood, his intense experiments in self-mortification, and his final founding of the order of Paulist Fathers. This sudden departure must have been the last straw for Almira, who soon afterward moved to Concord with the assistance of George Bradford, who had already left Brook Farm.

Now "restricted accommodations, the confusions and disorder" of instituting reform, as George Ripley put it, were starting to tear through others in the Community. Even Minot Pratt, one of the founders of the Farm, was talking of leaving. Somehow Ripley prevailed upon Mr. and Mrs. Pratt to stay on for another two years. Nevertheless trouble was in store.

The prospect of another poor harvest at Brook Farm

brought Albert Brisbane as a guest with a mission. With the help of Horace Greeley, *Tribune* editor and social reformer, he intended to turn Brook Farm into a living Fourieristic experiment—giant Phalanx, cooperative buying, community kitchens, lavish sun rooms, and all. Replacing their dances with long boring speeches, he lectured the Brook Farmers continually on the great benefits he had come to bestow on them. With money problems increasing and the ever-present threat of a meager crop hanging over his head, Ripley had no choice but to listen to Brisbane's propaganda.

In December of 1843 a variety of reformist sects gathered for a convention in Boston in the hope of organizing labor and industry for the good of all. It was here that Brook Farm became an experiment for Fourier's philosophy. With Brisbane's golden promises still sounding in his ears, George Ripley set about reorganizing the commune according to the new doctrine. Although Fourier's basic premise consisted of a law of natural attractions, of matching like with like, a man's tastes with his labors, the new element now attracted by the Brook Farm Phalanx (as it was christened) were not all of like mind and manners. Georgiana Bruce, one of its earliest settlers, confessed in letters to friends that she could no longer pretend to embrace all kinds of people; and she soon left. In early February a new constitution was drawn and ratified. Members were now to be reorganized into a system of Groups and Series under the leadership of elected chiefs.

Marianne Dwight, an enthusiastic young woman of

twenty-eight, had recently moved to the farm with her parents. "Despite the vulgar folk who had come to man the shops" (the "sweaty artisans" that Georgiana Bruce had found so difficult to live with), Marianne was determined to enjoy her new life. To her friend Anna Parsons, left behind in Boston, she wrote many long, gushing, and minutely descriptive letters that provide us with details about the Farm's Fourierist period that would have otherwise gone unrecorded.

In June of 1844 plans for the new Phalanstery—a giant communal building—were presented by Benjamin Rogers and accepted by the members.

Marianne found useful work in her talent for painting local wild flowers and selling her pictures to wealthy Boston ladies. Soon she was supervising other women in occupations like sewing and making knickknacks for the outside market.

George Curtis visited the farm and wrote to Isaac Hecker of his nostalgia for the good old simple days. "The place was so familiar, and yet so changed. The persons so different, the tone so different . . . but the wild, loitering busy leisure of old-times was far finer to my mind."

And no wonder, considering the varied types of applicants they now had to choose from: unskilled illiterates looking for free room and board, parasitic preachers with large families, traders offering cows, "three beds and bedding and ordinary things enough to keep a house." One man even promised three thousand dollars if he could be allowed to "labor and die in Association"—as the new movement was now called.

Ripley busied himself entirely with Fourierism, traveling around and spreading the word. By now fully imbued with Brisbane's high promises, he sincerely believed it could work. Orestes Brownson, an early member now turned Catholic, viewed the change with disgust. "The atmosphere of the place is horrible," he counseled Isaac Hecker. "Have no faith in such Association. They will be only gatherings of all that is vile to foster, and breed corruption." And he was not alone in his harsh judgment, for word had gotten around that Fourier had preached free love as part of his social system, and scandals about life at the Farm brewed everywhere.

By Fall of 1844 life had grown so difficult for the Farmers that food had to be rationed. Only certain people, for health reasons, were permitted items like tea, meat, and butter. As if that were not bad enough, Treasurer Charles Dana found the Association $804.04 in debt. Hopes revived, however, when it was announced that the official Fourieristic newspaper, *The Harbinger*, would be published at Brook Farm under the editorship of George Ripley. Things moved quickly and by March the Massachusetts legislature had granted them permission to incorporate. Moreover, although it hid and blocked off any view of the Eyrie, the new Phalanstery was under construction. From the start this building was ill-fated; workmen quarreled, newspapers and neighbors made fun of the anthill; and in spite of all the bustling new activity, a loyal old-timer like Amelia Russell could still write: "... now there seems scarce a pleasure left for me in Brookfarm. ... I think there is much real enthusiasm in some, but much that is false in others."

William Henry Channing, nephew of the famous older minister (who was now retired), used Brook Farm as a starting point for his Christian Socialist Campaign. Albert Brisbane, in the meantime, was turning an eye toward a new commune about to open in Red Bank, New Jersey—closer to New York City and his own interests.

It was as though the building of the anthill had released a Pandora's box worth of woes: first, in November of 1845 a smallpox epidemic from which, miraculously, all the victims recovered; then trouble with the building contractor; and, most depressing of all, a law suit instituted by Hawthorne for the balance of his investment plus damages. The writ was a harsh one, commanding the Sheriff of Middlesex County to "attach the goods or estate" of his old friend George Ripley for the value of eight hundred dollars. In addition to the original amount, Hawthorne—now married and soon to be a father—was applying "for other money ... diverse Goods, Wares, and Merchandise" with the warning of jail for Ripley if said monies were not paid.

Desperately Ripley turned to Brisbane and the central committee of Fourierists in New York. But Brisbane, always on the alert for new schemes and bored with unsuccessful ones, did nothing to help. In answer to Ripley's pleas he wrote: "You might as well undertake to raise dead men as to obtain any considerable amount of capital from the people here."

John Orvis and John Allen, two dedicated young men relatively new to the commune, vowed to save it. They packed off on a lecture tour throughout New England in search of subscriptions for *The Harbinger*. But in the heat of their excitement they did not take into account the bitterness of a New England winter, and the tour was largely a failure. It was as if the building of the Phalanx had brought with it a symbolic rain of plagues. A greenhouse undertaken in the hope of cultivating fine plants for marketing produced nothing that could be sold. William Henry Channing, once a friend of the Farmers, now despaired of the commune's continued existence. The threat of imprisonment hung over Ripley's head in the Hawthorne suit; people had fled during and even after the smallpox epidemic. Finally, as a culmination of all their disasters, the unfinished Phalanstery building burned to the ground. A workman had left an overnight lamp in an unfinished quarter of the house, unaware of a defective chimney. In the midst of a celebration in the Hive, the fire alarm was given. At first the Farmers thought it was a joke. Many of them had had misgivings about the new building and almost wished it would burn. Perhaps that is why nobody actually grieved at its collapse—nobody, that is, but Sophia and George Ripley, who saw in the ashes seven thousand dollars completely lost and the beginning of the end of their reformist dream.

To Anna Parsons in Boston, Marianne Dwight wrote: "There was a solemn, serious, reverential feeling, such as must come when we are forced to feel that human aid is of no avail, and that a higher power than man's is at work. I heard solemn words of trust, cheerful words of encouragement, of resignation, of gratitude and thankfulness, but not one of terror or despair."

Now the Brook Farm School had to be given up in favor of industrial work. Subscription money for *The Harbinger* did not come. And Hawthorne won his law suit. In March of 1847 a meeting was held for the purpose of disbanding Brook Farm. The minutes note that: "After a verbal statement from G. Ripley respecting the present condition of the Phalanx, it was voted unanimously that G. Ripley be authorized to let the farm for one year from March first for $350; and the Keith lot for $100 more, with such conditions and reservations as he may deem best for the interest of the stockholders."

The final business meeting was held in August 1847, at the end of which the few remaining members linked arms and went for a last moonlight stroll in the Piney Woods.

George and Sophia Ripley then moved to New York, where he was to assume the editorship of *The Harbinger* at its central office. The Association Union had decided to discontinue funds for lectures in the field in favor of emphasizing the role of the newspaper. Ripley, as general agent, was responsible for corresponding with and visiting the local unions. He devoted the paper to discussions of slavery, women's rights, and the cause of labor. And, although *The Harbinger* was soon to fail, the result of continued propagandizing for labor reform by men like Ripley, John Orvis, and John Allen was true public concern about the evils of the factory system and the development of Working Men's Protective Unions. The dreams of idealists like the residents of Brook Farm were on their way to becoming realities for later activists.

In the meantime members like John Dwight were devoting themselves to their chosen fields. In 1852, Dwight was to become editor of the *Journal of Music* in cooperation with the Harvard Music Society. His excellent critiques and articles served to elevate American musical tastes on a much larger scale than the work he had done at Brook Farm. George William Curtis became a famous man of letters when he took the post of first writer for "The Editor's Easy Chair" column in *Harper's* magazine. Marianne Dwight married John Orvis, who became a labor spokesman and editor of *The Voice of Industry*. Margaret Fuller went to Italy, married, and worked for the cause of Italian independence under Mazzini. On October 23, 1849, Isaac Hecker was ordained into the priesthood in Clapham, England.

Poor George Ripley remained optimistic in his Fourieristic cause. When in 1849 *The Harbinger* failed at last, he was reduced to nothing. Not one of his former friends offered him any assistance, although, like Charles Dana, now employed by Greeley at the *Tribune,* they had built their reputations under his guidance at Brook Farm. On April 10, 1849, in a letter to John Dwight, Ripley writes: ". . . but here I am a miserable invalid, all but a cripple, with no fruits of tough labors but disgraces and discontents."

Shortly afterward the town of Roxbury bought the Farm and converted it into a dwelling for the poor. George and Sophia continued to live in New York in a cheap one-room boarding house flat, where he wrote literary criticism for Greeley at five dollars a week and she taught school. Things took a turn for the better when it became apparent that Ripley's criticism was of a very high level indeed. Within six months he had doubled his salary, and in 1850 he joined *Harper's New Monthly Magazine* as a rather prominent literary figure. Sophia, turned inward by the hardships in her life, converted to Catholicism.

In 1852 Ripley, in collaboration with Bayard Taylor, compiled *A Handbook of Literature and Fine Arts*. In 1853, he was contributing pieces to *Putnam's Magazine*, and in 1857 he was on the way toward fulfilling his lifelong ambition of compiling a dictionary. For the first time since selling his precious library to Theodore Parker to keep Brook Farm running, George Ripley seemed destined for better times. But his selfless companion was not to share it with him, for in February of 1861 she died of cancer after a long period of suffering. Their old friend Isaac Hecker administered the Roman Catholic last rites. Alone and haunted with memories, Ripley moved to

Brooklyn and applied himself entirely to his work. By 1862 the first edition of his *New American Cyclopedia* appeared and was well received. His reputation as a scholar was now secure. It is almost as if in escaping his true vocation by trying too hard to help his fellow men in a way alien to his nature he had delayed the fulfillment of his real social purpose.

In 1865 he was married to a pretty German-American divorcee twenty years his junior. With his new wife he traveled abroad for the first time in his life to cover the Prussia-Austrian War for the *Tribune* and to record his experiences in London and Rome in a series of letters to that newspaper.

He returned to New York permanently in 1870 and remained there to become a prominent and respected literary light until his death at his writing desk on July 4, 1880.

In 1872 Brook Farm was bought by a Lutheran philanthropist who presented it to his church as an orphanage—which it remained for a long while after.

What happened to its blue-frocked, bearded young men and bloomered young women who danced every night in the Hive and picked flowers on Cow Island on Sundays? Some, like Orvis, went on to pursue their goals as reformers. But most, being artists, mystics, literary people, music scholars, and historians first and farmers last, moved on to work within the existing social order. The "sweaty artisans" also returned to work the land on farms of their own; the seamstresses returned to Boston to sew. As George Curtis, one of its more illustrious ex-members, later wrote:

> The effect of a residence at the Farm, I imagine, was not greater willingness to serve in the kitchen, and so particularly assert that labor was divine; but discontent that there was such a place as a kitchen. And however aimless life there seemed to be, it was an aimlessness of the general, not the individual life.

Brook Farm failed, but its Utopian promise lives still.

Isadora Duncan

*My art is an expression of life. My dancing is of
the imagination and spirit, not of the body. When
my body moves it is because my spirit moves it.*

Isadora Duncan believed in the supernatural, in the world
of fantasy and omens and astrology. During times of crisis
she would consult fortunetellers and then, in her own
inimitable way, she would reject all that they told her,
laugh, and sweep out of the room. Isadora was a true child
of Gemini, her astrological sign: half genius, half sensual-
ist. One part of her is represented by the artist, the
"mother of modern dance" who could stand for hours
concentrating before a long mirror before beginning to
dance. The other part, the more sensational and popular
one, could leave an audience of thousands waiting while
she chose to spend a day in the country with a new lover.
Isadora's single outstanding quality was her contradic-
toriness, the split personality symbolized by the astrological sign of the twins—a woman alternately vain and generous, exhibitionistic and frightened, a Communist and

an aristocrat all at once. But first and always—a dancer.

From the beginning Isadora never hesitated to go out and get what she felt was due her as a great genius. Even as a child in San Francisco she "decided that I would live to fight against marriage and for the emancipation of women and the right for every woman to have a child or children as it pleased her." She was a revolutionary even then, when at age six she opened her own "school of dance" in open rebellion against what she called the ugly and unnatural positions taught in the ballet class. One day her mother found her teaching a class of babies who could not yet walk how to wave their arms around. Being a progressive sort of mother, Mrs. Duncan encouraged the young Isadora in her venture.

Born May 27, 1878, to a ne'er-do-well father and a self-educated, bohemian mother who were soon after divorced, Isadora was the youngest of four children who, at an early age, were already accustomed to poverty and hardship. Yet she always recalled with pleasure those early years with her piano-playing rebel of a mother, her actor brothers, Raymond and Augustin, and her equally theatrical sister, Elizabeth.

> . . . it is certainly to this wild untrammelled life of my childhood that I owe the inspiration of the dance I created, which was but the expression of freedom. I was never subjected to the continued "don'ts" which it seems to me make children's lives a misery. . . . It was only at school that I suffered. To a proud and sensitive child the public school system, as I remember it, was as

humiliating as a penitentiary. . . . The dominant note of my childhood was the constant spirit of revolt against the narrowness of the society in which we lived.

It did not take long for Isadora to drop out not only from the conventional school life of a twelve-year-old girl but from the established norms of childhood altogether. Determined to become a famous dancer, she convinced her mother to accompany her to Chicago with the intention of joining a dance troupe under Augustin Daly, a powerful and important theatrical director of the time. Here, with no money and having lived for a week on nothing but tomatoes, the adolescent girl auditioned before the great Mr. Daly. But true to form, Isadora made sure that this was no ordinary audition. And as she was to do so often in her later life, she prefaced her dance with a lecture.

Isadora could never leave well enough alone. Like many inspired rebels, she felt compelled always to justify her own actions by endless theorizing and preaching. There was—in spite of her great European successes and her arty proclamations—something very much of the American high pressure salesman about her. Too often she would not rely on the greatness of her talent to advertise itself but rather on complicated and self-congratulatory explanations of her art. In later life it was this uncontrollable need to express everything she felt to all and any listeners that alienated her from the America which she loved so much.

Here, as an adolescent lecturing the nonplussed Augustin Daly in an empty Chicago theater, is one of the finest early examples of the uncontrollable Isadora:

> I have discovered the dance. I have discovered the art which has been lost for two thousand years. You are a supreme theatre artist, but there is one thing lacking in your theatre which made the old Greek theatre great, and this is the art of the dance. . . . I bring you the dance. I bring you the idea that is going to revolutionize our entire epoch. Where have I discovered it? By the Pacific Ocean, by the waving pine-forests of Sierra Nevada. I have seen the ideal figure of youthful America dancing over the top of the Rockies. . . . I am indeed the spiritual daughter of Walt Whitman. For the children of America I will create a new dance that will express America.

Perhaps more to put an end to the tirade than anything else, Daly offered her a bit in one of his New York musical productions. Convinced that Isadora was launched, Mrs. Duncan moved her little brood to New York City. She installed herself and her children in a bare Carnegie Hall studio, which she used by day for piano and elocution lessons, and by night—with mattresses thrown here and there on the floor—as the Duncan bedroom. In order to pay the rent it was often necessary to sublet the studio to other struggling "artistes" for several hours a day while Isadora, her mother, sister, and brothers jogged through the snow-covered Central Park to keep warm.

Isadora continued playing minor dance roles in Daly's

company; but it was high art, not music hall dancing, that she longed for. In order to earn a little extra money, she danced in the salons and on the lawns of New York society matrons, but most often they neglected to pay her, taking it for granted that the pleasure of their illustrious acquaintance was payment enough for the starstruck twenty-year-old dancer.

It is important to note that during the years of Isadora's unsuccessful New York career, the dance—outside of classical ballet and music hall high stepping—did not really exist as an art form. Dancers, like all other women of the period, were trussed, corseted, begowned. Even the free-wheeling Isadora, in photographs taken during this phase of her career, appears in a demure white lace costume with ribbons in her hair and pink tights and satin ballet slippers on her feet. Society ladies and other New Yorkers with artistic pretensions who attended her private studio recitals were delighted by this pretty dark-haired, blue-eyed young thing who pranced so sweetly to the strains of Mendelssohn. Mrs. Duncan played the piano and sometimes Raymond read poetry as an accompaniment to Isadora's dances.

When they ran out of rent money the Duncans dispatched Isadora to collect from her wealthy sponsors. Somehow, none of the Duncans could get around to working at anything other than their nonpaying artistic vocations in order to live. Isadora tramped up and down Fifth Avenue from mansion to mansion collecting only enough to get the family on a cattle boat to London. America obviously did not appreciate high art.

The situation, however, was not much better in London. Here, too, the family alternately starved in a bare studio or ate meager tea sandwiches on the lawns of the aristocracy, where Isadora performed her pretty dances. It was not until 1900, when the twenty-two-year-old Isadora decided to move to Paris, that she really "discovered the dance." Here, in the Louvre, she and brother Raymond spent days delighting in the study of Greek vases and bas-reliefs depicting dancing figures. In Paris, too, she sat enraptured at the outdoor performances of ancient Greek tragedies performed by Mounet-Sully, a renowned actor of the period. Led by the enthusiasm of Raymond and Isadora, the Duncan clan became so carried away with the glory that was Greece that they threw off their clothes and shoes and began wearing Greek-style tunics and sandals. To keep the shape of her beautifully formed feet, Isadora wore carpet slippers in their studio, a practice which she continued for most of her life. In her performances for the select Parisian intelligentsia, to whom she was introduced by her English poet and painter friends, Isadora now began to dance barefoot, wearing only a flimsy Greek tunic. In 1900 such a scandalous costume could only be compared to dancing nude.

Now as a true "daughter of Dionysus" and having cast aside all vestiges of her American Puritanism, Isadora truly began to create her own dance form. What she sought, as she stood for hours in almost Yogic trances before her studio mirror listening to the very pulse of life running through her body, was the elemental source of the dance itself. Abdicating the puppet-like formal movements of the ballet in order to dance to the music of her own soul, she made one of the most important discoveries since the beginnings of the dance. The work leading up to this discovery is described by Isadora in her autobiography, *My Life:* "For hours I would stand quite still, my two hands folded between my breasts, covering the solar plexus." What she learned (even before professional psychologists) and from then on tried to convey to others was that bodily movement is the first reaction to all sensory or emotional stimuli. She located the source of movement in the solar plexus, which she called "the crater of motor power, the unity from which all diversities of movements are born, the mirror of vision for the creation of the dance." In direct contrast to the preconceived movements of the ballet, Isadora's dancing expressed the primary emotions of love, joy, fear and sorrow. As far as she was concerned, dance now came to represent life itself; *her* conception of the free soul in the free body, expressing itself beyond the bounds of artistic or social conventions.

Isadora declared that her art was symbolic of one thing —the freedom of woman, the emancipation from "the hidebound conventions of American Puritanism." It was as the spiritual daughter of Walt Whitman that she determined never to marry but to take lovers as she chose and to bear children as she chose, without the restrictions of marriage. In her attempts to force her life style into a reflection of her free dance form, Isadora publicly boasted about her amorous adventures, made more speeches, and started on the path of reckless indulgence that was to characterize her entire life.

From Paris she and her family moved on to Berlin, Vienna, Budapest. Her reputation for dancing in bare feet and transparent tunics first brought the curious and, finally, the recognition of the serious critics as well. Never satisfied, always on the alert for new forms of expression, Isadora designed her own stage settings. She abandoned the clumsy, overcrowded scenery of the traditional theater for a bare stage draped only with long curtains of gray, soft greens, and blues that hung along the sides and rear. Accents of lighting dramatized the figure of the lone dancer onstage, whose stunning movements, according to admiring critics, suggested the ancient Greek myths.

In Berlin she improvised a new dance to *The Blue Danube* by Strauss, which was received with wild enthusiasm by her audiences. Isadora had finally achieved the artistic recognition she so desperately craved. Even the widow of the great composer Richard Wagner declared that Isadora was the only person capable of translating her husband's music into bodily movement. By the time she was twenty-six Isadora had earned enough money to fulfill a family dream: The Duncans now moved to Greece, and with the generous Isadora providing the funds, they proceeded to build a temple to the arts. Impractical as always, they forgot to make a study of the land site and found too late that there was no water to be had for miles. Nevertheless a cornerstone of the temple was erected and before their return to Germany the Duncans managed to relive the travels of Ulysses—tunics, sandals, and all—before the incredulous eyes of the Greek peasants en route.

The money gradually ran out (as it was always to do in Isadora's fluctuating career), and she returned to Berlin, together with her sister Elizabeth, in order to found a dance school for young girls. Under the auspices of the Grand Duke Ferdinand, the Duncans took a villa which they decorated according to Isadora's idea of a perfect dance school for young children—lovely blue-curtained nurseries and fairy-tale ribbons everywhere. Here she put her principles into action.

> We do not allow the child to make a single movement unless it knows why it makes it. I do not mean to say that the meaning of every motion must be explained to the child in words, but that the motion must be of such a nature that the child feels the reason for it in every fibre. In this way the child will become versed in the simple language of gestures.
>
> In the teaching of children to dance, three of their senses are exercised. Their eye is trained to note movement, their ear is trained to note time and harmony and their touch is developed to bring to them the knowledge of the existence of their whole body. This latter sense is the foundation of all the others, it is the foundation of existence; its development brings fuller life, greater activity and increased ability.

Another significant discovery of hers was the recognition that both dance rhythms and the body's response to those rhythms emerge from the pull of gravity. This concept was to revolutionize the entire art of choreography and dance for the future.

Putting her theories into practice, Isadora set about removing the little girl students from their families, stripping them of the suffocating garters, high button shoes, and stiff undergarments that even children then were forced to wear, and dressing them in sandals and free-flowing tunics. Her brother Raymond had by this time become a vegetarian of sorts, and Isadora—always quick to experiment with new and different cults—instituted a vegetarian diet at her school.

Before long, however, the old problem of money arose, and the little girls at the school saw less and less of their beloved Isadora and more and more of the tyrannical and unattractive sister Elizabeth. Although Isadora performed constantly during those Berlin years, her easy-going style of living, her love of parties, fine foods, and champagne kept her in perpetual debt. But the artist, the rebel, and the innovator in her could not be stilled. It was in Germany that she inaugurated what has come down to us as the modern bathing costume. Always conscious of her role as a leader in freedom for women, she appeared one day on the beach in a bathing suit of her own design. The good middle-class ladies in their long bathing dresses, black beach stockings, and rubber shoes were shocked at what they saw: a light blue crepe tunic, low necked, held up by small straps, with a short skirt exposing bare legs and feet. "You can well imagine the sensation I created," said the delighted Isadora. Enlightened aristocratic women immediately followed her example, and the modern bathing suit was born.

Isadora's exploits in nonconformism did not stop at fashion. When she found she was pregnant, she did not attempt to hide from her admiring public the fact that the father was Gordon Craig, the brilliant theater designer and son of actress Ellen Terry—and that he was not her legal husband. The relationship did not last long, but Isadora had her baby, a girl named Deirdre.

By the age of thirty-two Isadora found herself poor once again and her school on the brink of bankruptcy. This necessitated a move to Paris, where she was once again saved from financial ruin—this time by a millionaire lover whom she called "Lohengrin" and with whom she had a son named Patrick. Lohengrin offered to marry her, but—true to her principles—Isadora remained single. In the spring of 1913, when she was thirty-five and at the height of her glorious career, her two children were killed in a terrible car accident in Paris. The moralists who had condemned her in her own country were vindicated. Isadora, they said, had paid a terrible debt for her sins. It was this accident, the single greatest blow of her life, that pushed Isadora's reckless nature over the bounds of sheer rebellion. After deliberating between the possibilities of suicide or of never dancing again, during a lonely stay in Italy, Isadora decided that the only things now worth living for were devotion to her art and teaching children the creative movements she had discovered. Her art, from this point on, became infused with the tragedy she had suffered, and it now revealed new depths of talent that she had never tapped before. Audiences sobbed aloud when she danced the role of a grieving mother to Schubert's *Ave Maria*. The greatness of her art now began to rise higher and higher as her personal life and fortunes fell.

"I believe," she wrote, "that in each life there is a spiritual line, an upward curve, and all that adheres to and strengthens this line is our real life—the rest is but as chaff falling from us as our souls progress. Such a spiritual line is my Art. My life has known but two motives— Love and Art—and often Love destroyed Art, and often the imperious call of Art put a tragic end to Love. For these two have no accord, but only constant battle."

By 1914 the lovely villa outside Paris that Lohengrin had bought for her to use as a school was to be converted into a field hospital, for World War I was about to begin. Isadora gave birth to another child which died almost immediately in her arms. Wandering, always seeking a place in which to teach children to dance, she now returned to America in hope of founding a school in New York. It was with the war beginning in France that Isadora became aware of politics. Although it was in this area of life that she was perhaps most naive of all, she took up the cudgels of radicalism and revolution as easily as she had the liberation of women from their corsets. The year 1915 saw the beginning of her battle with America, her own country, which she dearly loved and continuously criticized and whose government and people eventually succeeded in isolating her, misunderstanding her work, and ignoring her into permanent exile. Dance critic Walter Terry describes Isadora's first tour of America during which she "proclaimed from the stage and in interviews her theories on the dance of the future, on the proper training of children, on her hopes for a school in America and even on love. She explained her opinions on morals and communicated to all her love of children, but the narrow-minded thought she was nothing more than a hussy, a fallen woman. They did not bother Isadora. She knew she was right."

But Isadora had dropped too far out of the American system to maintain its interest in her work. Her plans for a school in her native country were never realized. Instead, she was forced into heavier debt than ever before and, finally, into disbanding what was then left of her European school in Switzerland. By haranguing the rich who filled the expensive seats to see her dance, she succeeded in antagonizing even those few sympathetic people with enough wealth and power to assist her. Her self-destructive outspokenness ran an interesting pattern throughout her life. She was always ambivalent about wealth in that she would frequently put herself in a dependent position with wealthy patrons and then, almost in the same breath, would spit out at them, upholding the cause of the poor against them. In this way she man-

aged to sabotage all of her own plans for establishing her
Duncan schools of dance. Therefore, when she talked politics she often made a fool of herself. But when she danced
it she was eloquent. In New York she danced *The Mar-
seillaise* as a patriotic gesture to France, her adopted
country, which was just then at war. This tribute created
a genuine stir of emotion in America and came to sym-
bolize democracy and the rights of man everywhere.

Yet the woman who had created this stirring dance remained no more than a sensational hussy in the eyes of
most Americans. On April 10, 1915, she made a longer
speech than usual, and a rather prophetic one, too:

> I suppose that twenty-five years after I am dead they
> will come along and build an immense theatre, just
> about as ugly as this one, and try to start the work that
> I am doing now. They will build the theatre, but when
> they try to imitate me they will not know how to begin.
> They may get the same beautiful pictures, the same
> graceful movement of the limbs, the arms and the head,
> but the feeling will not be there.

In 1921, frustrated at the lack of interest in her art on
the part of what she now called "the materialistic Americans and Europeans," she accepted an offer to teach her
dancing to the children of revolutionary Russia. For the
next three years there began a series of naive hopes followed by a train of disillusionment and hardship that
Isadora could never have fathomed—not even in *her* wild-
est imaginings. In her true enthusiastic fashion, she

adopted the slogans and dress and idealism of what she thought represented the young Russian revolutionary government. Dressed from head to foot in red, loaded with trunks of food and clothing, and accompanied by her French maid and Irma Duncan, her adopted daughter and disciple, Isadora landed in Moscow expecting crowds of enthusiastic admirers and government officials. What she found, however, was poverty, starvation, and bedbugs; a struggling government concerned first with feeding its children and quelling counterrevolution, and lastly with Comrade Duncan and her dancing school.

Gradually, with the help of the sympathetic Lunacharsky, Commissar of Education and Culture, Isadora did open a Soviet dancing school for children in Moscow. During the part of the year when she and her pupils were not starving altogether, she did manage to teach. The remainder of the year was spent in begging bureaucrats for money and performing all over the Soviet Union (often without a place to sleep and stranded without funds to continue her tours) in order to keep the school going. All was not entirely suffering—she was received with unbounded enthusiasm by Russian intellectuals and workers alike, even in the farthest outlying regions where the peasant classes had barely begun to adjust to their new-found freedom. She had the pleasure of hearing "bravos" from Lenin himself; she led thousands of Russian children in a patriotic tribute to the revolution which she had created to the stirring *Internationale*, the Soviet national anthem; and it was in Russia too that in

1922 she broke her resolution against marriage by becoming the wife of the young, mad revolutionary poet, Sergei Essenin.

Driven by the continual need for funds, she went on a tour of Europe and America in the company of her young husband. (He was twenty-seven, she was forty-four.) The entire trip consisted of nothing but tragedy, drunken scenes with the alcoholic Essenin, bad press, wild spending sprees, and enormous debt. The once great idol of Europe was now seen by all but a few remaining loyal admirers and friends as nothing more than a shrill, heavy, aging Bolshevik given to drinking and jealous scenes with her cruel, baby-faced husband.

Her trip to America proved to be a catastrophe. Having been held up at Ellis Island by government officials as a possible Bolshevik spy, banned in Boston for indecent exposure, branded a naked dancer/Communist by the mayor of Indianapolis, and ultimately deprived of her American citizenship altogether, Isadora told reporters:

> I have been driven out of America. The United States is insane on the questions of Bolshevism, Prohibition, and Ku-Klux-Klan. In that land of the free there is no more freedom! The American papers printed details of my personal life, what I ate, what I drank, the people I associated with, but never once said a single word about my art. Materialism has become the curse of America!

Isadora discovered that a mixture of art and politics could not work. She vowed never again to return to the land of her birth, and she never did.

After a disastrous stay in Europe she and Essenin returned separately to Russia, where they were soon after divorced. From 1923 on, her fortunes and those of her Moscow school declined so drastically that she was driven once again to flee to Western Europe in the hope of obtaining money. Her frantic letters to Irma Duncan, in whose hands she had left the school, reflect the downward rush toward what in three short years was to be the end.

Berlin, November, 1924:
I have signed three contracts and been swindled three times. . . . When the time came, the agent didn't have the money for the R.R. tickets. They are all swindlers.
I cannot move from here! The hotel has refused to serve us food for the last four weeks. An American friend brings me a slice of roast beef a day, but he has no money either.

Isadora's sister Elizabeth and her brother Raymond, although they were relatively close at hand, deserted her then, too. As if all this was not bad enough, the once idolized Isadora could not get a visa to remain anywhere in Europe. In December of 1924 she writes from Berlin:

Every country has refused me a visa on account of my "political connections." What are my political connections? Where are my political connections, I would like to know?
I am utterly stranded and lost here in a very hostile city. I haven't a single friend. . . .
Perhaps I. [Ilya Schneider, her dance school manager

in Moscow] had better get on a plane and come here
and save me, otherwise you will soon be sending a
wreath for my funeral.

Friends scraped together a few hundred dollars for her
and with this she traveled to Paris. After many unsuccessful negotiations to set up her dancing school there, much
starvation, and—when money did miraculously fall from
somewhere—the usual lavish champagne suppers for
young lovers, Isadora went to Nice. Here she moved in
temporarily with her brother Raymond, who had established himself as the head of a vegetarian cult of craftsmen
who specialized in handwoven fabrics and carpets and
dressed in Greek togas and sandals year round.

Within a year Isadora had tired of Raymond's ascetic
hardwood benches and his green salads. Despite her
egalitarian sentiments she much preferred plush pillows
and vintage champagne. To afford her high tastes, Isadora needed money, and when an American publisher
promised her a huge sum, she agreed to write her memoirs. From the time that her children were killed, Isadora
was always restless and hardly able to sit still, so it was no
surprise that at first she proved unable to write her autobiography. Nor was it a surprise that she ran through the
publisher's advance without handing in so much as a
chapter heading.

The picture had become a faded, unpleasant one. Isadora, the once sylph-like dancer with the lithe body, was
now at forty-seven a heavy, often tipsy, aging woman who
had lost her admirers, her friends, and the dream of her

professional life—her dancing school. Still she retained her sense of loyalty and generous good nature, which revealed itself when her ex-husband, Sergei Essenin, committed suicide in their honeymoon hotel room in Leningrad. When newspapers depicted him as a wild, drunken monster and their marriage a catastrophe, Isadora answered in his defense:

> *New York Times.* January 2, 1926—
> Yessenin despaired of life in a world where so few persons cared about art. He must have taken his life during a passing fit of madness. My consolation lies in the thought that his poems will survive his tragic death.

Then, although she herself was destitute and living on the handouts of close friends, Isadora turned over substantial sums from Essenin's royalties to his mother and sister in Moscow.

From time to time she tried to write her memoirs or to start performing again. Having moved from Raymond's studio, she established herself in a small combination theater-studio in Nice, where she gave private performances among the draperies and soft lighting that had marked better times. Some now said that she kept the sunlight out of the rooms in order to hide her wrinkles from her young lovers. She indulged in wild automobile trips and flirtatious encounters with young men of all social classes. She received bad publicity by making what seemed like dramatic but pretended suicide attempts. One such attempt, during which she walked into the sea by moonlight at a party, is characteristic of her depressed condition. Instead of thanking the man who saved her from drowning, she merely looked up at the moon and said: "What a beautiful scene that would have made for the movies." She seems, at this point, to have removed herself from life entirely. Often she talked of suicide with her friend and companion Mary Desti. But then again some money would turn up, or a new friend, or a fine bottle of champagne, and Isadora would begin to look up again. Good times were always accompanied by the urge to dance.

It was in such a mood that she returned to Paris in 1927 to give what has been called the greatest performance of her life. And her last. Wrapped in her customary shawls, she danced her most beloved dances—among them the stirringly tragic *Ave Maria* and Wagner's Funeral March from *Siegfried*. The theater rang with the exultant cries of critics and friends alike. Armed with the acclaim she had sought and successfully renewed, Isadora returned to Nice.

On the evening of September 14, 1927, Isadora wrapped herself dramatically in a long fringed red Chinese silk scarf embroidered with birds and embarked on a ride in an Italian sports car. The chauffeur, a young man to whom she had taken a fancy, started the engine. Isadora called back over her shoulder to the friends she had left behind, "Good-by, my friends, I'm off to glory!"—without noticing that one end of the long scarf had caught in the spokes of the rear wheel. The car pulled forward.

Mary Desti cried out for her to pick up the shawl, but it was too late. The shawl, too tightly wound about the hub and spokes of the wheel, had broken her neck. Death came to Isadora instantly.

What she left behind were no dancing schools in her name and no particular identifiable dancing techniques, although her stamp is indelibly impressed on the modern dance movement and even to some extent on the classical ballet. Yet she was an *original* in the truest sense of the word, and when she died there was no one to copy her. She did not want imitators and once said: "Others began to imitate me, not understanding that it was necessary to go back to the beginning, to find something in themselves first. . . . Unless your dancing springs from an inner emotion and expresses an idea, it will be meaningless."

Isadora's influence, however, manifested itself more strongly forty years after her death, more so in the liberalizing of social attitudes, and particularly in the liberation of women. Of chorus girls in a musical comedy as early as 1922, she said: "It was ghastly to see beautiful young girls come out on the stage saying meaningless words and making meaningless gestures, when they could have been taught to be a force to the nation."

And of a woman's role in life: "One cannot make plans for life, or rules for marriage. Life comes, and one lives, each day. I am opposed to marriages. I believe in the emancipation of women.

"There are many who think, apparently, that life is a series of extremely boring habits which they call virtues.

I do not believe in putting chains and a padlock on life. . . . Most Americans are hypnotized by a wrong idea of life, brought to this country by the Puritans."

In her own life style, tragic as it often was, Isadora personified the liberated woman. In her art she combined ingenuity, emotion, and dedication—but never at the expense of the self-expression which was the hallmark of this unusual woman. She freed children from the unnatural and repressed movements of the body they were subject to in so-called dancing schools all over the world. Sandals and free-swinging dresses, short bathing suits rather than long black woolies and ugly rubber shoes at the shore—all of these are symbols of Isadora's one-woman revolution against convention. But more important, as her impresario S. Hurok has written: "She brought sunlight and fresh air into the lives and thinking of all of us; she cut the bonds of spirit as well as flesh. . . . The touch of her free spirit is on the bodies and minds of young America today."

Thomas Merton

The monk is not simply a contemplative who
"shares the fruits of his contemplation." He is one
who is on a pilgrimage "out of this world to the
Father" and while remaining in the present life he
is a sign of the world to come. . . . The monk re-
tains his own perspective and his own horizons—
which are those of the desert and of exile. But this
in itself should enable him to have a special under-
standing of his fellow man in an age of alienation.

There is a Zen Buddhist tale of a young monk who asks
his master how he will know when he has achieved enlightenment. The master replies: "When you first come
to the monastery, mountains are mountains, rivers are
only rivers, and trees are trees. Then, after you have been
here and have meditated for a while, you will discover
that mountains are no longer mountains, rivers no longer
rivers, and trees no longer trees. But when you are enlightened and ready to leave the monastery, you will look
around you and once again you will discover that mountains are mountains, that rivers are rivers, and that trees
are trees."

So too, for those special men whose hearts are filled with spiritual longing even right here in our own noisy, technological midst, it is sometimes necessary to "die" to this world in order truly to find it. Thomas Merton was such a man; perhaps more than a man, perhaps—like one of his heroes, the poet William Blake—a kind of earthy saint whose quest took him beyond the bounds of any monastery and any organized church. His life began on the outskirts of convention when, on January 31, 1915, he was born to a bohemian couple in the south of France. His father, a New Zealander, was an artist; his mother was a nonconforming American agnostic individualist who died when Tom was only five and his brother John Paul still a baby. Merton's early years were spent alternately in traveling with his father on excursions to Provincetown, Massachusetts, and Bermuda, and living on Long Island with his mother's very upright, very middle-class conformist parents. So there was really no one place in which he was raised; the faces of his childhood never remained the same for long, and from his earliest years Thomas Merton adjusted to the rootless life of "the loner." The youth found his friends among the beach birds and lush Bermuda flowers that his father loved to paint. It was here, in this enforced isolation from the conventional life of other boys, that he probably developed not only the sense of religious solitude that was to color his later life but the perceptive loneliness of the poet that haunted Merton the monk until his death.

In 1925 his father, now a successful painter, returned from a long stay in Europe and, leaving John Paul with his grandparents on Long Island, brought Tom back with him to France. But here, too, the boy remained isolated, living as an outsider in the town of St. Antonin in southern France, suspected by his classmates of being that most horrible of creatures—an Englishman—and periodically getting his ears tweaked during recess hours. No wonder that he chose to live alone, populating his mind with heroic fantasies of himself as the fourth and bravest member of the *Three Musketeers*.

"As a child, and since then too, I have always tended to resist any kind of a possessive affection on the part of other human beings—there has always been this profound instinct to keep clear, to keep free . . ." he was to write later in his confessional autobiography, *The Seven Storey Mountain*.

On the outside he was meek, giving in easily to the will of adults and to their authority—if a bit sulky in disposition. But this façade of gentleness was exchanged for a more aggressive one at the outset of adolescence when the young Tom made a self-conscious decision to resist to the death the will and opinions of others. Something of this early adolescent rebelliousness against the system—any system—later echoed behind the adult decision to lead his life as a contemplative monk at a time when the world seemed to call more than ever before for action; and even beyond that, as a radical poet-monk with Buddhist leanings.

Removed from his French tormentors and sent to a proper English boarding school in the Midlands, Merton found himself growing more withdrawn than ever before, hardened to the spirit of life around him, cool and above it all; that is until the death of his father left him to confront his sad fate—truly alone this time. By now eighteen and free to choose whatever he wished to do with his life, he dedicated himself to having a good time and to reading everything he could get his hands on. He went at it with the same kind of drive and fervor that he was later to exhibit in his religious conversion.

It is a commonplace that the greatest saints have often been the greatest sinners. Indeed William Blake tells us (as he did the young student Merton) that the road to heaven leads straight through hell. For Tom Merton, the self-styled intellectual, this largely entailed (as it has for so many student "sinners") great drinking bouts, "fast" women, and much reading of free-thinking authors. Although today such a judgment of sin might strike us as a bit prudish (as it later did Father Merton himself), this life style was enough eventually to upset the delicate balance of the unhappy young man. Enrolled at Cambridge and living on a small inheritance administered by an English uncle, Merton only once briefly experienced the God-longing that was to characterize the rest of his life. It happened while he was on a holiday visit to Rome. Here, in a vision of his dead father, the young man underwent the first crucial revelation of the dark and lonely state of his soul:

> The whole thing passed in a flash, but in that flash, instantly, I was overwhelmed with a sudden and profound

insight into the misery and corruption of my own soul, and I was pierced deeply with a light that made me realize something of the condition I was in, and I was filled with horror at what I saw. . . . And now I think for the first time in my whole life I really began to pray—

But this proved to be a short-lived conversion, soon after exchanged for a mild political activism in which Merton flattered himself into believing he was a Marxist. In 1934 during a period similar to ours in its ferment— student unrest and threat of war—on the advice of his uncle, Merton left for America and entered Columbia College. As a self-styled radical his Marxism took the form of attending a few campus rallies, swearing never to join the army in a gymnasium pledge, and attending a radicals' party in a Park Avenue flat. This phase of political activism was short-lived. Yet, immature as it was, it apparently formed the kernel for his later social concern and for the humanitarianism that underlies all of his writings. This was later to evolve into a moral rather than a political radicalism in which the poet-monk would identify with beats and blacks, poets and the young, and, perhaps most of all, with the poor and downtrodden of the earth. It was as Father Merton that he would be the first important active Catholic theologian in the peace movement of the 1960s—often despite the censorship of conservative church authority.

Friends at Columbia remember him as an earthy, humorous, and extraordinarily intelligent young Englishman. When alone, however, Tom, the outgoing intellectual and bawdy cartoonist from Cambridge, was struggling with metaphysical questions in the basement stacks of the college library, seeking—even in the midst of his very worldly life—"the possibility of real, experimental contact with God." That search framed the beginning of the transformation of a radical intellectual into a God-hungry mystic. It was at Columbia that he read Frater Wiger's translations of Buddhist texts, and here too that the abstractions of Oriental mysticism merged for him with the more accessible image of Christ. While at work on his Master's thesis on William Blake (by his senior year in 1938, in imitation of his English professor and friend Mark Van Doren, Merton had decided to continue on in literature with the hope of becoming a great writer and teacher) he was led to conclude that ". . . the only way to live was to live in a world that was charged with the presence and reality of God."

The dark and dusty underground of the Columbia library stacks seems an odd place in which to "get religion." It may be that the books Merton was reading at the time —many of which were edited by Jesuits and which often made reference to medieval Christian mystics—reminded him of his childhood in France. There Tom the schoolboy had been surrounded by glorious cathedrals and by the simple Catholic faith of the farming people who lived in the medieval town of St. Antonin. Nevertheless it was at this crucial point that a Hindu monk entered Merton's life and gave him the decisive push toward religion.

Bramachari had been sent by the abbot of his own religious order in India to attend the Chicago World Congress of Religions and World's Fair. Since he had to beg his way over to America alone and on foot, by the time Bramachari arrived both the Congress and the Fair had long been disbanded. He remained in Chicago, wearing his turban, white cloth robe, and Keds sneakers, long enough to learn English and to obtain a doctorate in philosophy from the University of Chicago. The wife of a friend of Merton's, who had been a student in Chicago, invited Bramachari to New York. It was in the crowded Grand Central Station that Thomas Merton first laid eyes on the odd little monk who was soon to advise him to turn his life to God, and to do it by way of reading Saint Augustine!

After this meeting Merton's search for knowledge of mysticism through books began to give way to the need for actual experience of religion itself. One quiet Sunday morning he found himself timidly entering Corpus Christi, a little Catholic church near Columbia. He had taken the first step. Within a year, in that same church, he had converted to Catholicism. Yet despite his new-found happiness in his faith, and despite the fact that some of his closest friends had followed his example and become Catholics, too, Merton felt that something was lacking. It was at this point that he began to sense certain contradictions in himself and in the life he was leading. Before long he was tormented with doubts about the conflicts between his ambitions, his desires, and his worldly pursuits, and his growing need to be always meditating on God and things of the spirit. It was in 1939, with the war in Europe already begun and a year after his "conversion of the intellect," that Thomas Merton knew that he was to live for God alone. Pondering constantly on the collective evil of men as a cause of the war that was by this time growing closer and closer to America, he concluded that it was the evil of the individual soul that created the external horror of war. He was not thinking now of the youthful antics of his Cambridge "sins," but rather formulating the basis of his belief that it was the greed and selfish corruption of human nature itself that were responsible for the terrible conflicts of the world. What could he as an individual, a humanist intellectual who believed in God with all his heart, do to eradicate these evils in himself and point the way for others? There seemed, at this moment in his life, no other answer except to become a priest.

He was sitting on the floor of his Greenwich Village apartment one early morning after a long night of talking and drinking with friends. Outside, in the world, Germany had invaded Poland. The group of young students had already embarked on a new discussion when Merton suddenly and simply blurted out: "I want to be a priest." It was not really a decision but more like something that one remembers one has forgotten to do, something that *must* be done. He left the apartment and went to an early morning Mass in a West Village church close by the docks of the Hudson River. There, with the Mass already in full progress, as he entered the answer struck him clearly: "Yes, I want to be a priest, with all my heart I want it. If it is Your will, make me a priest—make me a priest."

For most men reaching this point, life would fall into a proper religious pattern: entrance into an Order as a novice, ordination, and assumption of priestly duties either in teaching, community church work, or the like. But not for Thomas Merton, whose crusty intellectual exterior had been completely exploded, leaving in its place a mystical longing that was to continue to burn at white heat all his life. Organized religion never satisfied this longing for him. He ultimately found himself gravitating toward the Trappists—a Cistercian Order, founded during the Middle Ages in France. This religious order demands total retreat from the world, permits no talking among the brothers, requires that the monks fast more than half the year and perform hard physical labor daily when they are not at their prayers.

During the two years he spent preparing first for entry into the Franciscan Order and then for permission to join the Trappists, he joined a group of Catholic lay workers who had dedicated their lives to the poor people of the slums by actually living and working in their midst. It was here in the Harlem of 1939–1940 that Merton obtained a first-hand glimpse of the condition of the black man in America. It was a glimpse that immediately transformed him into a "civil rights" activist and a continued fighter for the black man's cause long before the sit-ins and

strikes that became the hallmark of the 1960s. His appraisal of the race situation then, sadly, remains similar
to the one he wrote twenty-four years later in *Seeds of
Destruction*, a collection of essays and letters comment-
ing on the downward course of the modern world.

[1940] Harlem itself, and every individual Negro in it,
is a living condemnation of our so-called "culture." Harlem is there by way of a divine indictment against New
York City and the people who live downtown and make
their money downtown. . . . Harlem is, in a sense, what
God thinks of Hollywood. And Hollywood is all Harlem
has, in its despair, to grasp at, by way of a surrogate for
heaven. . . . No, there is not a Negro in the whole place
who can fail to know, in the marrow of his own bones
that the white man's culture is not worth the jetsam in
the Harlem River.

[1964] The time has come when both White and
Negro have been granted, by God, a unique and mo-
mentous opportunity to repair this injustice and to re-
establish the violated moral and social orders on a new
plane. . . . We have this opportunity because the Negro
has taken steps which make it possible. He has refused
to accept the iniquity and injustice of white discrimina-
tion. [Should the white man remain deaf and blind to
the awakening of the Negro to his rights, the Negro]
will no longer be the gentle, wide-eyed child singing
hymns while police dogs lunge at his throat. . . . He will
become a Samson whose African strength flows omi-
nously back into his arms. He will suddenly pull the
pillars of white society crashing down upon himself and

his oppressors. . . . At the present time the word "patience" has been used and abused to cover every kind of inaction, foot dragging, double-crossing, and political shilly-shallying so that when a person says "patience" to the Negro now, the Negro simply dismisses his statement as meaningless.

Although they come from an "isolated" monk, these are certainly not the words of an otherworldly isolationist. They characterize the vigorous tone of everything he was to write after entering the monastery—his poetry (which, oddly enough, only blossomed soon after the decision to join the Order), political and social essays, even his good-humored open letters to his friends.

The greatest trial of his life was about to begin when, on December 10, 1941, Merton entered the Trappist Abbey of Gethsemani in Kentucky. In order to understand the course of his emotional life after ordination, it is important to remember that the very heart of the Trappist rule is the destruction of the individual personality in total submission before God. Penances of the flesh, such as sleeping on a wooden plank or on a heap of straw on a cold stone floor, fasting and solitary prayers make up much of the novice's life. Thomas Merton submitted willingly to the physical penances; he had made the choice himself. Yet something within him resisted; some*one* within him needed desperately to hold onto his personality and God-given talent in order to survive. And it was probably this "other"—as he later called it—Merton the writer, who refused to be cracked by the rules and who was also responsible for the terrible depression that seized him after ordination.

In 1944 his first book of poems was published, and although in 1945 the abbot permitted him to continue writing and even to continue publishing his works, Merton was constantly tormented by the war between the two men who occupied his body: the quiet, contemplative monk, and the outgoing, communicative poet.

> By this time I should have been delivered of any problems about my true identity. I had already made my simple profession. And my vows should have divested me of the last shreds of any special identity. But then there was this shadow, this double, this writer who had followed me into the cloister. . . . He is still on my track. . . . He still wears the name of Thomas Merton. Is it the name of an enemy?

Merton fought with his "enemy" and attempted to stifle him by choosing to remain in the monastery, for he needed withdrawal in order to contemplate God, and perhaps even to go on writing as well. He stayed, but it was not always a smooth or a happy stay. At times, according to friends, he grew desperate, unable to communicate with his fellow monks or with a new abbot, and lived almost entirely through his poetry and lonely prayers. Finally after bouts of illness and despair over the conflict between his own ideal conception of the spiritual life and what he often found to be the real rigid and materialistic practice in the monastery itself, in 1961 he persuaded the abbot to let him live as a hermit in a tiny cottage on the grounds of the abbey. Isolated two steps further from the world, Merton now began his working day at two in the morning and performed the office of the Mass alone. The appearance of his autobiography in 1959 had made him world famous, so that by the time he had removed himself to his heatless, toiletless hermitage he was already corresponding with figures from every walk of life in all parts of the world: writers like Hemingway and Pasternak, politicians, civil rights workers, nuns, and even Buddhist monks in India.

Under the influence of solitary meditation, the old interest in Oriental mysticism flared anew and, by means of a correspondence with Dr. D. T. Suzuki, the Buddhist scholar, he undertook the study of Zen Buddhism. With great effort and at great cost to his physical health, Merton managed to juggle his two lives. He acted as an adviser to novice monks for ten years and, although he didn't much like the job, inspired the young men of the Order with fresh liberal ideas about their obligations to God and their fellow men.

> To be a solitary but not an individualist: concerned not with merely perfecting one's own life (that, as Marx saw it, is an indecent luxury and full of illusion). One's solitude belongs to the world and to God. . . . Solitude has its own special work: a deepening of awareness that the world needs. A struggle against alienation. True solitude is deeply aware of the world's needs. It does not hold the world at arm's length.

For my own part, I am by my whole life committed to a certain protest and non-acquiescence, and that is why I am a monk. Yet I know that protest is not enough —is perhaps meaningless. Yet that is also why protest and non-acquiescence must extend to certain conceptions of monasticism which seem to me to be simply a fancy-dress adaptation of what we are claiming to have renounced.

Inevitably such statements and a growing tendency on Merton's part to openly condemn reactionary forces both in his own church and in American politics brought the wrath of the authorities down upon him. Sections of his *Secular Journal* were deleted, certain liberal Catholic magazines were forbidden him, and a book he wrote advocating world peace was suppressed altogether. His tone became increasingly radical, but, contrary to what one might expect, his religion deepened. However, by the mid-1960s, although the Catholic church always remained his religious home, his writings and personal interests began to lean more heavily Eastward. In 1965 he edited a book on Gandhi's philosophy of nonviolence in which he clearly expressed his own growing conviction that it was the duty of a true man of God to speak out:

A society that lives by organized greed or by systematic terrorism and oppression (they come to much the same thing in the end) will always tend to be violent because it is in a state of persistent disorder and moral confusion. The first valid political action in such a society

then becomes *non-cooperation* with its disorder, its in-
justices, and more particularly with its deep commitment to untruth.

And he joins with Thoreau in urging men to civil disobedience in a time when

> . . . there are very dangerous ambiguities about our
> democracy in its actual present condition. I wonder to
> what extent our ideals are now a front for organized
> selfishness and systematic irresponsibility. . . . If our
> affluent society ever breaks down and the façade is taken
> away, what are we going to have left?
>
> Thoreau's idleness . . . was an incomparable gift that
> America has never really learned to appreciate. (In-
> dustrious and affluent America, busy making more
> money than ever, has little time for him. . . .)

By 1964 Merton saw the monk's role much differently
than he had in *The Seven Storey Mountain*. "True, in
the past I have been much more inclined to that kind of
'contemplation' which looks into the ground of one's
being. . . . My personal vocation tends to be solitary and
reflective: but one learns over a period of years to go beyond the limits of a narrow and subjective absorption
into one's own 'interiority' (ugh)." Spurred by the harsh
confrontation with the nature of reality in his practice of
Zen, Merton saw that ". . . there are times when this
shelter is itself deceptive. . . . Genuine communication
is becoming more and more difficult, and when speech

is in danger of perishing or being perverted in the amplified noise of beasts, perhaps it becomes obligatory for a monk to try to speak."

Now with assassination and riot a part of the everyday life of America, Merton struck out not only against all forms of tyranny but against tacit assent to it as well. He even went so far as to question conservative elements in the church he loved so deeply: "If in practice the function of organized religion turns out to be nothing more than to justify and to canonize the routines of mass society; if organized religion abdicates its mission to disturb man in the depths of his conscience . . . then it deserves the most serious and uncompromising criticism."

It was in this mood that Merton headed East to participate in an ecumenical council of Catholic and Buddhist monks, hoping to "bring back to my monastery something of the Asian wisdom with which I am fortunate to be in contact—"

In a lightning-fast tour that took him from Calcutta to New Delhi (where he met with the exiled Dalai Lama, high priest of Tibet), to Darjeeling (where he lived in the forest as a Buddhist hermit), to Thailand, Merton seemed to be searching for a way of fusing the religious experiences of East and West in order to open at least the beginnings of a dialogue between them, and in the hope of avoiding world disaster. It was in Bangkok on December 9, 1968, that he died of accidental electrocution from an electric fan.

From boyhood his search for enlightenment had taken

Thomas Merton all the way around the world, then out of it and into religious retreat, and finally, as a poet, social critic, and Zen mystic, back into it again. In the twenty-seven years he spent as a Trappist monk he wrote over thirty books, innumerable letters, articles, and poems. Thomas Merton was a monk living in the twentieth-century diaspora as he called it, thrust out of the medieval church structure and into a new kind of monastic world where it was necessary to perform his spiritual work in close association with ordinary men, sometimes at the cost of ceremonies and practices that had outlived their needs.

". . . It is no longer possible to fall back into a comfortable and spiritual realm that is consoling and delightful," he wrote in a letter to a Greek poet, "and man must realize that he is not just a 'soul' . . . because we live in an age where the much more difficult task is not that of having a pure soul but also that of spiritualizing matter."

In *Cables to the Ace*, a book of complex poems published in 1967, Merton agonizes over mechanized America, its wars, its advertising, its dehumanization through mindless technological advancement. Then in a strange metaphorical leap he talks of going to the East to die "in a distant country." Perhaps this time Thomas Merton really knew and was prepared to leave the world for good.

Dick Gregory

This is a revolution. It started long before I came into it, and I may die before it's over, but we'll bust this thing and cut out this cancer. America will be as strong and beautiful as it should be, for black folks and white folks. We'll all be free then, free from a system that makes a man less than a man, that teaches hate and fear and ignorance.

Richard Claxton Gregory was born on October 12, 1932, in the black ghetto of St. Louis. Former street arab and college dropout just about a week before graduation, he rose to become the first black man ever to see his name on the ballot in the race for president of the United States. His rags to riches story would have been just another example of the young black boy from the ghetto making it big in sports or show business—the only real openings for a black boy growing up in the fifties—except that Gregory had more on his mind. When he was very little, his mother took him to see the neighborhood fortuneteller. The old lady claimed to see a star bursting forth from the center of the boy's forehead, and she predicted brilliant things for him. Gregory believed her. "All my life I've wanted a parade. Just me and those people waving to me."

As a child, however, it was not as president or as spokesman for his people that he fancied himself. Richard, the welfare case boy who slept in an overcrowded bed with five other brothers and sisters, who listened to the rats run by at night, who froze in winter and starved in summer, dreamed mainly of two things: having his absent daddy come home and being a fireman.

"One time I bought an old raincoat with hooks instead of buttons, and a pair of old hip boots. I hid them in the cellar. Nobody knew I had them. Whenever I wanted to feel good I'd put them on and walk around the cellar, pretending I was putting out fires, running up ladders to save people, catching people in my net. . . . Sometimes, before I knew better, I used to think my daddy was a fireman somewhere, saving people and saying nice things to kids."

To add to her pitifully small welfare check, Gregory's mother worked as a housekeeper for a wealthy white family. The Gregory children resented having to bring themselves up while some strange white children enjoyed their mother's cuddling and feeding. While her white charges played in their spacious gardens or went to exclusive private schools, young Richard Gregory was working in the downtown tavern as a shoe-shine boy. There, from the drunks, gamblers, and prostitutes, he received an education of a different kind. Once, after being kicked in the face by a white man, he was given five dollars by the bartender, who felt sorry for him. It was a hard way to earn money but Gregory thought himself lucky. While his mother sat home at night gazing out of the window and hoping his father would come home, the young boy was out selling papers or stealing gifts for his family from the local five and dime store.

Early on, Dick Gregory learned how to take care of himself. First he learned when and how to lie. A little later on, at school, he learned from a hostile white teacher how to accept humiliation without crying. Then he learned the most painful lesson—the truth about his daddy. This took place on one of the rare occasions when his father chose to come home. Big Pres, as he was called, walked in one night wearing a fancy silk suit and sporting a pocket full of bills. He made many promises to his children, cried for forgiveness from his wife, and soon after became drunk and abusive. Dick hadn't believed any of the promises. He had covered his head with a blanket and hardly spoken when his father walked in that night. But when he saw the man beating his mother, he could no longer contain his feelings.

"I got up off the floor and I walked into that kitchen. Big Pres was sitting at the table with his face in his hands, and Momma was standing over him, stroking his head. They both were crying. I took down the butcher knife off the wall, the big one with the black handle, and swung at his head. Seen plenty of people swing knives in the taverns and I knew how to cut. Swung right at his head, everything I had, I swung for every kid in the whole world who hated his no-good Daddy." Big Pres left the house and did not return again.

By some strange quirk, the bitterness inside the boy found a release in humor. From the bigger, tougher boys on the street who picked on him, who said that the Gregory kids were on relief and that their clothing and bodies smelled bad, he learned the powerful self-defense of a joke. Before his attacker had the chance to open, Gregory sprang into action. If the subject concerned the overcrowded beds in his apartment, he would say something like, "Yeah, we got so many sisters and brothers sleeping in one bed, that when I get up to pee I have to leave a bookmark to keep my place."

Talking and talking fast and funny became Dick Gregory's defense against the shame and anger of being rejected, fatherless, and poor. He managed to talk his way through high school and, in spite of the fact that he never studied and could never finish a book, he became an important figure to his classmates. Thrust into an all black school predominantly attended by middle- and upper-class youngsters, Dick once again shrewdly made his way. There it was no longer a question of escaping. He would have to join and prove himself somehow in order to keep the respect of the clean, well-dressed sons and daughters of prominent black families. Always the big negotiator with the glib tongue, sophisticated in the ways of the ghetto, he established himself as the mediator between the few toughs on the fringes of school life and the boys and girls of the upper crust. Even teachers depended on him to break up fights. He, in turn, depended on his fast and growing repartee to get him out of dangerous confrontations.

"Baby, you'd better kill me quick. If you don't I'm gonna steal those cool shoes you wearin'," he would say, rolling his eyes at the boy who had him pinned up against the wall. He little expected then that the experiment in nonviolence would prove invaluable in what were to become almost daily eye-to-eye confrontations with white sheriffs in Alabama. But heroism was not on Gregory's mind at high school. Succeeding with the wealthy, light-skinned black girls in his class seemed most important then.

Ashamed because he could not take showers at home or change his clothes daily, he decided to join the track team when he learned that athletes were permitted to take showers at school every evening after practice. That was supposedly his reason for starting in sports. But it is interesting to note that he chose track, a sport which gave him the opportunity to run far away from the fears of inferiority and failure inside.

I don't think I ever would have finished high school without running. It was something that kept me going from day to day . . . to look forward to going a little faster and a little longer at three o'clock. And I felt so good when I ran. . . . I could think anything I wanted while I ran and talk to myself and sometimes I'd write

stories on "My Favorite Daddy" and "What I'd Buy
With a Million Dollars." . . . Nobody would point to
me and say I was poor or crazy; they'd just look at me
with admiration and say: "He's training."

At seventeen he was running, working in the furnace
pit of a munitions factory, going to school, and playing
the bass drum in the marching band. Dick Gregory really
felt that star in his forehead begin to glimmer. Soon it
was shining more brightly than he had ever hoped or
imagined. He began winning all the track meets. People
at school stared and waved, and girls got to know his
name. He steeped himself in the luxury of fame, of being
a "celebrity." The blow came when he found out that
he was only a "local celebrity," and a "local *Negro* celebrity" at that. This was the background for Dick Gregory's first direct move toward civil rights action. The
Scholastic Record Book for 1951, a published collection
of high school athletes, did not contain any reference to
the Dick Gregory who was then winning all the segre-
gated track meets. Out of personal frustration, he vol-
unteered to act as a marshal at a demonstration by parents and children against overcrowded school conditions. He was questioned by reporters who subsequently
labeled him as the leader of the demonstration.

"Nothing much happened right away, but the next
week the high school cross-country program was integrated." Gregory beat the white champion and was em-
braced as a great, first-class black athlete by whites now

too. Events were preparing him to fulfill the promise of the black boy's American dream. He became president of the school class (using his influence with the school hoodlums to obtain votes) and received an athletic scholarship to Southern Illinois University. College proved at first to be more of high school glory on a grander scale. Here he became captain of the track team, orchestra drummer, variety show actor and comic, but something was wrong. Biggest man on campus, Dick Gregory could not eat out with his teammates nor could he sit in the orchestra section of the local movie house.

"In high school I was fighting being broke and on relief, and each Saturday I'd go out and recharge my batteries, be a hero for another week. But in college I was fighting being Negro."

One day Dick Gregory sat down in the orchestra section of the town movie theater and was told to go upstairs. He continued to sit there each time he came to see a film in spite of pleas, threats, and conferences with the manager. Finally nobody asked him to go upstairs. The local people even got used to seeing him there and they no longer stared. He was sitting in the orchestra section of that same movie house when his mother died of overwork in St. Louis at the age of forty-eight. That omen marked the beginning of many bitter sit-ins which were later always to bear the tinge of death.

By 1954 when he was drafted into the army, Dick Gregory had cultivated a taste for telling funny stories in front of audiences and hearing them laugh. Now he could relax and talk about his ghetto upbringing at college shows; he could defend himself against the humiliation of prejudice as he had against the neighborhood toughs —by getting the joke out before the attacker struck. People laughed and Gregory began to take himself seriously as a pretty funny fellow, a fast talker rather than a fast runner. In the army he perfected his delivery sharply enough to win all the Special Services talent show awards.

In 1956 he returned to Southern Illinois. But the bloom had worn off; he found himself flunking courses and drifting along. College was not what he wanted. It had given him a token taste of freedom and only a token acceptance. If he could not be accepted as a man for himself only but had to keep proving his social worth as an educated black hero, according to white man's standards, he would take nothing. Just before graduation Dick Gregory sent himself a telegram guaranteeing him twenty-five thousand dollars a year as a comedian in Baltimore. Chucking the entire little empire he had built for himself, he left for Chicago with no degree and without looking back.

With only a few friends to help him along, he started searching for work. It might sound romantic to give up a secure and tangible place in the world for an intangible abstraction like self-respect, but it is never easy. Gregory discovered this after months of no work and little food. Still believing in his own comic gift, he began to frequent black night clubs. Handing the master of ceremonies a borrowed five dollar bill to let him perform, Gregory managed to get an audience. His following was small at first, but soon he was doing so well that the owner of one club asked him to be weekend master of ceremonies for ten dollars a night. The comedian-in-training had struck gold. Like the track star of before, he was in training again. "For the first time since high school, I got that thirsty taste again, waiting each week to go out and crush the world. Only now I didn't have to beat anybody. I had to make people happy. Every day during the week I'd be . . . buying comedy records, buying joke books, watching television, listening to people, going to the library and digging into musty old books of humor."

Dick Gregory was being recognized. Among his fans at the local night club was Lillian Smith, who worked at the University of Chicago. The shy young woman could hardly believe it when the great celebrity himself asked her for a date. But again, compelled by the drive to move on and up, driven by the glowing star in his forehead, he turned away from the club and resigned when the owner refused to raise his salary.

"When I quit the Esquire I had the same funny feeling in my stomach I had when I left college with nowhere to go. Everything, everyone was behind me."

On eight hundred dollars borrowed from Lillian Smith and other friends, he opened his own club in a suburb of Chicago. The Apex Club was a shabby, haunted-looking room that provided him some temporary good luck and a place in which to hone his comic gift. Yet although it was a happy period for him, the brief life of the Apex

Club came to a close when the weather turned bad and people stopped coming.

Gregory had convinced himself that his friend Lillian was a rich out-of-town girl. He was therefore not prepared, when he came to her for another loan, to find that she had not only given him all her savings but that she was expecting his baby as well. They were married that winter, and while Dick continued to struggle with the Apex Club in Chicago, Lillian remained with his sister in St. Louis. In July he became both the father of a baby girl and ex-owner of the Apex Club: "a part of something ethical and honest and decent, a place . . . that—for us—had been something like a home."

It isn't often that a man's life assumes the character of an organized play with acts and scenes closing, curtains falling, and beginnings, middles, and ends. But Dick Gregory's life seems strangely to have fallen into the perfect dramatic pattern. Few men have the courage to face change, even if that change involves growth. Perhaps he had adapted to the rapid, often desperate changes that are part and parcel of ghetto life. Perhaps it was the street boy's shrewdness and adaptability that enabled Dick Gregory to close one door and immediately prepare himself to open the next one.

In the summer of 1959 Gregory brought his wife and infant daughter to Chicago. Lillian again went to work at the University. In his fifty-dollar Plymouth, the baby wrapped in a blanket on the front seat beside him, the aspiring comedian made the rounds of agents and club owners in search of a place where he could be funny. After a great deal of driving he at last obtained a small spot in a large black-owned club. He studied the popular black comedians and was again confronted by the old college problem, this time in new dress. The fact remained that a black comedian was black first and funny second; much the same as a track star was black first and fast second. For a long time Gregory pondered the problem of the white man and the black man in humorous confrontation. "That white customer in the Negro club is filled with guilt and fear. . . . When I step up on that stage, in *their* neighborhood, some of them are going to feel sorry for me because I'm a Negro. Those who feel sorry might laugh a little at first. But they can't respect someone they pity, and eventually they'll stop laughing. Those who hate me aren't going to laugh at all. . . . I've got to be a colored funny man, not a funny colored man. . . . I've got to make jokes about myself, before I can make jokes about them and their society—that way, they can't hate me. Comedy is friendly relations."

In January of 1961, when a white comedian fell ill, Dick Gregory had a chance to test his strategy at the Playboy Club in Chicago in front of an audience of frozen food executives from the South!

His strategy apparently worked, for overnight Dick Gregory was catapulted into national prominence as the first socially significant black comedian. It was he who injected an entirely new image of blackness on the television screen: Dick Gregory became the first black comedian asked to sit down on a television talk show. Before long, after the spending sprees and the big hotels and the elegant clothing, he found that not only were people laughing at his jokes, but that they were listening to him as well. From this new position, Dick Gregory could demand that nonsegregation clauses be placed in his contracts. As a celebrity who called his own signals, he could take time off and perform in benefits for CORE and NAACP. There seemed no limit to what he could do once the star in his forehead had burst forth to shed its radiance everywhere he went. "And I kept pushing my material further, more topical, more racial, more digging into a system I was beginning to understand better and attack more intelligently. I was speaking at more and more rallies and benefits now, getting to know and talk with the civil rights leaders—Roy Wilkins, Whitney Young, James Farmer, Martin Luther King—beginning to realize just how large and complicated this problem is."

Shortly after the first exhilarating dip into national prominence, Dick Gregory realized that even *this* was not what he was after. It was almost as if everything he had been working toward, to find a better life for himself, his wife, and his children, had merely been a prelude for something bigger and deeper than what he had seen from a distance. He had succeeded in ridding himself of the stench of the ghetto, and he had run far enough away to satisfy his own ego—but what of the millions of other little Dick Gregorys who were still shining the shoes of white men in taverns back home? And what of the memory of his mother who had died of working so hard to raise white people's children and gotten nothing of the great American dream in return?

Fame and night clubs and cheers did not last long enough or loud enough to drown out the cry of fellow black voices in Mississippi. Fame, for Dick Gregory, now became synonymous with responsibility. He discovered then that it was truly the time for him to act, but to act for others.

Local authorities in Mississippi had refused to ship federal surplus foods to poverty-stricken areas (mostly black) in retaliation for the voter registration drives that had taken place there.

> Hell, as long as any man, white or black, isn't getting his rights in America I'm in danger. Sure I could stay in the night clubs and say clever things. But if America goes to war tomorrow would I stay home and satirize it . . . ? No, I'd go overseas and lay on some cold dirt, taking the chance of dying to guarantee a bunch of foreigners a better life than my own Momma got in America.

Commitment to those people in the back woods of Mississippi came in stages. At first he sent money, chartered a plane for the food to be sent, even spent a few days and nights there himself. Yet he had fears about actually "getting out on those streets and marching against bullets and dogs and water hoses and cattle prods."

By 1963 he had conquered all fears for his own life. Facing a church filled with local people in Greenwood, Mississippi, people who were willing to march out into the open for their rights and risk what little they owned in the world, people without his chance to fly back home to Chicago, hurried the decision. Dick Gregory agreed to lead them in a nonviolent demonstration for voting rights. And it was as bad and as dangerous as he had imagined: bombs flying through the windows of churches where he spoke, death threats, friends being shot in the back, being jailed in Birmingham, and the ever-present sheriffs spitting in his face and screaming "Nigger" at him. It was hard to remain nonviolent. It was also growing increasingly harder to maintain the double life as activist and "most successful Negro stand-up comedian of the last half-century." In May, he canceled an important night club engagement in San Francisco in order to accompany Medgar Evers in a Jackson, Mississippi, demonstration. Gregory had an evil premonition of death when he left that night. Accustomed to the violence he had encountered in the streets of the South, he assumed that it would be himself or someone close. He had hardly considered that it was to be his infant son, left safely at home in his crib, who would take sick and die. The tragic premonition that day was to cast its blot even further, not only in the murders of his friends Medgar Evers and Martin Luther King but in the killing of innocent black children seated in Southern churches and schools.

Dick Gregory now found himself on the receiving end

of hate mail, crank telephone calls in the middle of the night, and the most outrageous commercial attempts on the part of "friends" and "ministers" to capitalize on the loss of his son. Something about all this touched a new nerve inside—a more defiant, a less frightened one.

"A scared Negro is one thing. A mad Negro is something else. I had always gone down South scared. But in September, when I went down to Selma, Alabama, Whitey had a mad Negro on his hands." A new element had been added to his growing first-hand acquaintance with American prejudice: the awareness that the liberal North could be all the more insidious in its brand of racial hatred. In a demonstration for better schools in Chicago, he was arrested and treated more brutally than he had been down South. At least the Southern white man had put his cards on the table and spat directly in his face. But in his home town it was much more subtle than that, taking the form of police harassment, framed convictions, and unseen public officials pulling invisible strings when the demonstrations became too public.

The turning point came on a Friday night in a church in Selma, Alabama—the recognition of his real goal, the true function of that forehead star.

I feel it when I stand in front of a crowd of people hungry for freedom, and I feel it when we march down a street for our rights. Hot water seeping up into a cold body, that dry taste in my mouth. The monster. But it's not content to beat some mother's son in a foot race any more, and it's not satisfied to make people laugh and love me. Now it wants some respect and dignity, and it wants freedom. It's willing to die for freedom.

But the thirst for freedom often conflicts with the traditional values of the Establishment. Increased activism in the civil rights movement brought Dick Gregory farther away from the stereotyped image of the show business Negro. For many white night club owners and television executives he was too hot. Militancy in the mid-sixties had not yet become fashionable. Nobody was doing documentaries on the ghetto then, and H. Rap Brown was still a young, nonviolent SNCC student that no one had heard of—except perhaps for the old, illiterate black people he was teaching to read in preparation for voter registration.

But by that time Dick Gregory was already too busy to think about not being funny on television. Those days found him more concerned with restraining himself from punching the policeman who had just spat in his wife's face during a peaceful downtown march. He was then, too, turning toward vegetarianism in a protest against *all* killing and experimenting with a Gandhi-type protest fast against repression and injustice of all kinds. At Christmas in 1964 he personally engineered a project in which thousands of turkeys were flown down to the poor of Mississippi so that many who had never eaten a turkey before could have one now.

And he grew busier and busier articulating the new

thoughts and observations that had been forming in his mind. He wrote books and began to take an interest in national affairs, economic problems of all people—even the policeman—and he started to speak out against the Vietnam war. Most important, he provided a burgeoning new political movement—consisting of the young, the black, and the disgruntled liberal intellectual—with a sharp, insightful, and often witty view of what was going wrong in America. Beyond that, Dick Gregory also proved himself capable of prescribing remedies for those wrongs.

There is a great social revolution going on in America today. And the wonderful thing about this revolution is that it is not black against white. It is simply right against wrong.

The day you join the revolution is the day you will quit hating.

His friend and collaborator Reverend James R. Mc-Graw notes:

No demonstration is too small, no demand upon his time or personal finances is too great. He has marched with a handful of pickets in Greenwood, Misssissippi, and he joined thousands of marchers in Montgomery, Alabama. And all at his own expense. His participation in the struggle for human dignity has cost him over a million dollars in travel expenses and cancelled book-ings. Add to that his innumerable legal expenses and you have a commercial rendering of the high price of freedom.

Dick Gregory started to point out things at the cost of risking his popularity as a comedian, at the cost of losing all the money he had earned, and even at the cost of his life. During the troubles in the Watts ghetto of Los Angeles in the summer of 1967, he was shot and wounded. Yet in spite of his own professed nonviolence he has seen deeply enough into the kind of frustration that makes violence inevitable.

Acts of civil disobedience, whether they are nonviolent demonstrations or riots, are attempts to get America's attention. If I am talking and you want to get my attention, you will say in a normal voice, "Dick Gregory." If I pay no attention to you, you will say in a much louder voice, "Dick Gregory." If I still refuse to listen to you, you will stand in front of me so that I cannot avoid seeing you. If everything else fails to get my attention, you will finally grab me and shake me and say, "Dick Gregory, listen to me." The chances are I will listen to what you have to say. The throwing of bricks in the ghettos of the nation is the shaking of the foundations of America so that she must listen to the grief of her black children.

By her refusal to listen and act, America has caused moderate Negro leadership to be rejected by the black ghettos.

His own approach is more in keeping with that form of civil disobedience practiced by men like Gandhi, Thoreau, and the Reverend Martin Luther King.

> Persons who engage in acts of civil disobedience
> should be willing to suffer the penalty imposed by the
> unjust law, both to demonstrate the injustice of the
> law and to show a respect for law and order when it
> operates within a framework of justice.

This kind of thinking has led him into jail for sit-in demonstrations, into fasting himself down to toothpick proportions to protest the war in Vietnam, and to risking the fortune he once thought he wanted so much.

"I don't believe in money. I dump mine. I don't want it. I don't need it. I don't even want insurance. I tell my wife if I die tomorrow and there's no insurance money to raise my kids on she's gonna have to bring them up on wisdom and knowledge." A far cry from the high school boy running around the track from eight in the morning until six at night dreaming of how to spend a million dollars.

Oddly enough, stepping out of show business and into the maelstrom of social reform made him even more popular than before; so popular, in fact, that in 1968 he was able to campaign for the presidency of the United States! Running on an independent peace and freedom ticket, he even managed to get his name on the ballot in some states, while in others he waged a write-in campaign. Nobody would have been more surprised than Dick Gregory if he had won. Nevertheless, he, like no other candidate white or black, brought to the surface those very issues that had been simmering directly underneath for so long.

Before the college riots and the assassinations Dick Gregory the social gadfly was telling America all about what ailed it—without any sugar coating. Because he considered himself more of a free lance statesman than a politician and could therefore not lose one way or the other, he could point out, for example, that:

America is a violent teacher. We commit murder in the name of government by permitting capital punishment. That is violent. We induct young men into the armed services, instruct them in the use of weapons, teach them to kill, and tell them that it is honorable to wage war. That is violent instruction. We place violent people in positions of "peace officers" with cattle prods and tear gas as their tools for keeping the peace. . . . We permitted churches to be bombed and children disintegrated. We have burned babies in Alabama and in Vietnam. Is it any wonder that the violent whirlwind haunts America with the echo "Burn, baby, burn?" America has sown the wind of violence and she shall reap the whirlwind of destruction.

It is true that I am very bitter and very angry. I do not hate America, but I despise the moral pollution which infects the national body. . . . America is my home and I do not plan to move anywhere else.

His antidotes to the "moral pollution" he sees here are the simplest, the oldest, and the hardest to find anywhere since the world began: for power to give way to compassion, for extending knowledge and food and medical assistance to the underdeveloped nations of the world rather than weapons and military personnel. His idea of government at home consists of community organization and citizen participation in an atmosphere where, like the income tax laws, the civil rights laws would be rigidly enforced.

> I would urge private industry and universities to develop projects which would meet the problems of depressed urban and rural areas and submit their proposals for government approval. . . . In times of war, the private business sector and the government work hand in hand through government contract. The same should be true of the War on Poverty.

Even though he did not win the election, on March 4, 1969 (the original date of Inauguration until the Roosevelt Administration changed it), Dick Gregory was inaugurated as president-in-exile. An inaugural ball was held in a Washington hotel and the "president" made a humorous speech before a crowd of invited luminaries from all walks of life. For many young people Dick Gregory still is the underground president of the United States. Both during and after the campaign Gregory the dropout went back to college. He traveled from one end of the country to the other—often working in two distant places in the course of one day—lecturing and joking and carrying his message to the students. He made records and did one-night stands in small clubs across the country. He appeared at rallies of every kind and he continued to demonstrate and land in jail and be beaten and abused in the cause of his struggle.

His comedy consists of topical material with a bite, interspersed every so often with a serious social reminder like the fact that ninety million people have been killed in wars since 1900; or that America has found it easier to land a man on the moon than to land one black family in a white suburb.

Dick Gregory is a man who cannot stand still. Even now he is changing. Just as he seems to settle down into one setting—be it show business comic or demonstration leader, statesman or traveling sociology professor—he moves on to something else. When everyone thought he was busy on the college scene, he surprised people by returning for extended night club dates. In a New York interview after a two week engagement at the Village Gate, when questioned about the change in tactics he said that he needed to pay the rent. Then again he could just as well be planning something new and entirely unexpected. It would be unlike Dick Gregory to stay anywhere for very long while injustice still exists around him.

"I achieved fame and fortune, both childhood ambitions, which were seen to be meaningless once attained. . . . But the real champion, I have come to understand, is the man who has risen to the crest of life's highest purpose—singular and complete devotion to serving one's fellow man."

Watch him.

Bibliography

Allen, Gay Wilson. *The Solitary Singer*. New York: New York University Press, 1967 (paperback).

Anderson, Charles, ed. *American Literary Masters*. Vol. 1. New York: Holt, Rinehart & Winston, 1965.

Brooks, Van Wyck, *The Flowering of New England*. New York: Dutton, 1952.

Curtis, Edith. *A Season in Utopia*. New York: Nelson, 1961.

Derleth, August. *Henry David Thoreau: Concord Rebel*. Philadelphia: Chilton, 1963.

Dickinson, Emily. *Selected Poems*. Introduction by Conrad Aiken. New York: Modern Library, 1924.

Duncan, Irma. *Duncan Dancer: An Autobiography*. Middletown, Conn.: Wesleyan University Press, 1966.

Duncan, Isadora. *My Life: An Autobiography*. New York: Award Books, 1969 (paperback).

Gregory, Dick. *The Shadow That Scares Me*. Edited by James R. McGraw. New York: Doubleday, 1968.

———. *Write Me In!* Edited by James R. McGraw. New York: Bantam Books, 1968 (paperback).

Gregory, Dick, with Robert Lipsyte. *Nigger: An Autobiography*. New York: Dutton, 1964.

Harding, Walter. *A Thoreau Handbook*. New York: New York University Press, 1959 (paperback).

Hawthorne, Nathaniel. *The Blithedale Romance*. Introduction by Arlin Turner. New York: Norton, 1958 (paperback).

Hoff, Rhoda. *Four American Poets—Why They Wrote*. New York: Walck, 1969.

170   *Bibliography*

Merton, Thomas. *Cables to the Ace.* New York: New Directions 1968 (paperback).

———. *Conjectures of a Guilty Bystander.* New York: Doubleday, 1966.

———. *Gandhi on Non-Violence.* New York: New Directions, 1965 (paperback).

———. *Mystics and Zen Masters.* New York: Farrar, Straus & Giroux, 1967.

———. *No Man Is an Island.* New York: Harcourt, 1955.

———. *The Secular Journal of Thomas Merton.* New York: Doubleday, 1969 (paperback).

———. *Seeds of Destruction.* New York: Farrar, Straus & Giroux, 1964.

———. *Selected Poems.* New York: New Directions, 1967 (paperback).

———. *The Seven Storey Mountain.* New York: Harcourt, 1948.

Padover, Saul. *The Genius of America.* New York: McGraw-Hill, 1960.

Schneider, Ilya Ilyich. *Isadora Duncan: The Russian Years.* Translated by David Magarshack. New York: Harcourt, 1968.

Terry, Walter. *Isadora Duncan.* New York: Dodd Mead, 1963.

Thoreau, Henry David. *The Portable Thoreau.* Edited by Carl Bode. New York: Viking, 1966 (paperback).

Untermeyer, Louis. *Makers of the Modern World.* New York: Simon & Schuster, 1955.

Whicher, George. *This Was a Poet.* Ann Arbor: University of Michigan Press, 1965 (paperback).

Whitman, Walt. *The Whitman Reader.* Edited by Maxwell Geismar. New York: Pocket Books, 1955 (paperback).

Wilde, Larry. *The Great Comedians Talk About Comedy,* New York: Citadel, 1968.

Index

Terry, Walter, 119
Therrier, Alex, 14–15
Thoreau, Cynthia (mother), 7
Thoreau, Helen (sister), 7
Thoreau, Henry David, 1, 56;
  and brother, 9–10, 11; childhood of, 7; and Emerson, 3,
  5–6, 8, 10–11, 18; final illness of, 20–21; jobs of, 7,
  8–9, 10, 12, 18–19; opinions
  of, 2–3, 16, 17, 19, 20; personality of, 1–2, 5; philosophy of, 13–14, 142, 163;
  at Walden Pond, 2, 3–4,
  13–18; and women, 3–4, 10;
  writings of, 1, 2, 4, 6, 9–10,
  20, 21, 22
Thoreau, John (father), 7
Thoreau, John (brother), 7, 9,
  10; death of, 11, 15
Thoreau, Sophia (sister), 7
Tolstoi, Leo, 17
Transcendentalism, 51, 80;
  feelings about, 10, 24
Transcendentalist Club, 2, 78;
  members of, 77, 89
Trappists, 137, 139, 145
Traubel, Horace, 74

Wadsworth, Rev. Charles, 38,
  39; and Emily Dickinson,
  26, 32, 34, 35
Walden (Thoreau), 4, 19
Walden Pond, 2, 3, 4, 6, 13,
  14–15, 17

Washington, D.C., 26, 71;
  Whitman in, 58, 59, 61, 62,
  63, 69
*A Week on the Concord and
  Merrimac Rivers* (Thoreau),
  10, 15, 18, 19, 20
West Roxbury, Mass. (later
  Roxbury), 79, 80, 104
Whitman, George (brother),
  58, 59, 61, 65, 69
Whitman, Jeff (brother), 69
Whitman, Jess (brother), 65
Whitman, Walt, 37, 110; acceptance of, 67–68, 71, 73,
  74, 75; and America, 41–43,
  48, 49, 55, 72, 73, 75; beliefs
  of, 45, 50–51, 51–53, 74;
  and Civil War, 58–61, 62–
  65; illnesses of, 68, 69–70,
  73–74; jobs of, 45–47, 48–
  49, 51; learning of, 45–46,
  51; lecture tours of, 71–72,
  73; vision of self, 41, 43, 47,
  54–55; writings of, 43, 45,
  49, 50, 53–55, 57, 58, 61–
  63, 64, 66–67, 68, 72–
  73
Whitman, Walter (father),
  44, 46
Whittier, John Greenleaf, 30,
  47
Wilkins, Roy, 157
World War I, 118

Young, Whitney, 157